STRATEGIC PUBLIC RELATIONS

STRATEGIC PUBLIC RELATIONS

10

PRINCIPLES TO HARNESS THE POWER OF PR

JENNIFER GEHRT AND COLLEEN MOFFITT
WITH ANDREA CARLOS

Library of Congress Control Number: 2008910592
ISBN: Hardcover   978-1-4363-8725-5
               Softcover   978-1-4363-8724-8

To order additional copies of this book, contact:
Xlibris Corporation
1-888-795-4274
www.Xlibris.com
Orders@Xlibris.com
51981

CONTENTS

ACKNOWLEDGMENTS

E very great accomplishment involves the participation of more than just one or two individuals. We would like to thank a group of very special people who devoted their time and attention to help us by providing insight and feedback for this book even while they were busy founding companies, developing exciting new products and services, and essentially changing the world with their efforts:

- For insights about developing great relationships, we'd like to thank Caroline Boren, Alaska Airlines; Keith Lindenburg, Deloitte; Bruce Patton, Harvard Negotiation Project and coauthor of the best-selling book *Getting to Yes*; Charlie Gillette, Knowledge Anywhere; Andrea Mocherman, SNAPin Software; Steve Brodie, Skytap; and Lee Weinstein, Lee Weinstein & Associates.
- For straightforward input about strategic PR approaches, we want to recognize Paul Thelen, Big Fish Games; Kathy Cripps, Council of Public Relations Firms; Richard Tait, Cranium; Rick Murray, Edelman; Don Davidge, Melodeo; Rick Romatowski, formerly with Open Interface North America; Mark Weiner, PRIME Research; Harvey Bauer, Tideworks Technology; Blake Cahill, Visible Technologies; Dennis Kaill, formerly with Microscan Systems Inc.; and Dean Owen, World Vision.
- On working with the media, analysts, and other topics related to media relations, we appreciate the insights provided by Mark Lodato, Arizona State University; Iain Gillott, iGR; Catherine Smith, Linden

Lab; Mason Essif, Ogilvy Public Relations Worldwide; Matt Slagle, Sony Online Entertainment; Brad Stevens, Starbucks; Diane Dimond, veteran journalist and author of *Be Careful Who You Love: Inside the Michael Jackson Case;* and Kevin Essebaggers, WWTV/WWUP.

- For providing keen insights about a broad range of topics covered in our book, we'd like to thank Susan Johnston, Clearwire; Elaine Long, Coaching Action; Stan Sorensen, Egencia, an Expedia Inc. company; Michelle Goldberg, Ignition Partners; Glenda Dorchak, Intrinsyc; Bill Strelke, formerly with Knowledge Anywhere; Katherine Lagana, LexisNexis; Anthony Bay, MOD Systems; Leigh Fatzinger, On Message; David Perry, Seattle Children's Hospital; Jennifer Seymour, Seattle Children's Hospital; and Brad Hefta-Gaub, Sweat365.com.

We would also like to recognize Mary Catherine Lamb and Kelli Jerome for their talents and dedication. They helped keep us focused and provided savvy input to ensure that we accomplished what we set out to do with this book. Every member of our team at Communiqué Public Relations has contributed to this effort throughout the years. We would like to especially recognize Paulette Zimmerman for her dedication to ensure that our clients experience what we talk about in this book. We are also extremely grateful for Don Campbell's and Gayl'e Morrison's help over the past years.

We also want to thank our family and friends for their support. In particular we want to thank John Moffitt, a wonderful husband and brother in-law, for his understanding, humor, and encouragement.

Most important, we would like to acknowledge our parents, Kathleen and John Gehrt. They have given us the greatest gift of all by sharing their wisdom, love, and encouragement to pursue our dreams and achieve more than we ever thought possible.

FOREWORD

When I started my career almost three decades ago, the Internet didn't exist, there was no cable TV, and the microcomputer revolution was still an ambitious dream. Although I recognized the important contribution of public relations toward a company's success, I had yet to discover how critical this discipline would become over time.

The role of PR is much richer and more nuanced now than ever before. And as the balance of power in the world of media shifts away from traditional outlets to new communication channels over the Internet, the role of PR continues to evolve at a rapid clip.

Never before have organizations been watched so closely. And never before have the consequences of their decisions led to such varied implications and scrutiny, shaping how they're perceived by the broader world. Executives who once kept up with the news by opening up the morning newspaper are now starting their workdays logging on to Google to sift through a large compilation of media coverage, peruse video and social networking sites such as YouTube and Facebook, and scan comments posted on a vast number of blogs. It's a very different and complex world.

In this new communications climate, keeping your business moving ahead poses a huge challenge, and reading *Strategic Public Relations* provides an invaluable strategic advantage. Over the years, Jennifer and Colleen have refined and perfected their PR practices, in the process becoming leading PR experts who play an integral role in ensuring that their clients achieve a competitive edge. *Strategic Public Relations* combines shrewd insights from two decades of experience with firsthand lessons from today's foremost PR experts to help you achieve extraordinary breakthroughs for your organization.

Unlike most other public relations books on the market, which focus on developing press releases and other PR tactics, *Strategic Public Relations* is both strategic and timely. The book shows you how you can use this rising discipline more effectively to advance your organization's most important business objectives. It also explains how to keep up with the rapidly changing communications landscape, helping you to leverage public relations to its fullest potential even as new technologies emerge and people use them in ways no one ever imagined.

No matter where you are in your career, you'll find *Strategic Public Relations* to be smart, entertaining, and insightful. It's a must-read for anyone committed to making a difference in their organization and the broader business world.

—Brad Stevens, former vice president of U.S. marketing, Starbucks

INTRODUCTION

I magine you just built a gigantic new windmill. Your windmill spins proudly above your home, catching the wind as it whirls. It can be seen from miles away. It looks impressive from a distance. Yet there's a fundamental problem: nobody has bothered to connect your windmill to a generator so that it produces the electricity you need to sustain your way of life.

Although they don't realize it, the vast majority of today's companies approach public relations in much the same way. Regardless of size, most organizations have some kind of PR program in place. Yet few use PR to its maximum potential. Like a windmill that's not hooked to a generator, most companies expend a lot of energy on PR at the tactical level while failing to harness the full strategic power it can produce. For PR to generate maximum impact, it must be based on sound strategy that targets the customers you need to reach and furthers the specific business goals you want to accomplish.

Strategic Public Relations is about helping you use PR to achieve maximum impact. It's about showing you how you can take your PR program from the tactical to the strategic to propel your business toward fullest success. Whether you're a seasoned business executive, a middle manager or PR practitioner, or even a relative newcomer to the business world, you already know that the business landscape is changing faster than a lightning bolt flashes through the sky. Most likely, you're already working to implement different ways of doing things in response to the hyperactive digital age in which we live. So why must you also change the way you approach PR?

The truth is that until recently you could get away with a tactical approach to PR. Granted, it wasn't ideal, but you *could* get away with it, especially if you relied on advertising and other marketing disciplines to push your business forward.

But that's not the case anymore. Why? Because the way we communicate is undergoing a seismic shift. The Web is colliding with the old ways of doing things. It's shaking and rolling the communications terrain as we know it, pushing us all off-balance. As the colliding subsides and the forces settle, PR is rising up to a new level of importance. In the new world order, relegating PR to the tactical is a dangerous mistake. Frankly, it's putting your company at risk.

A SEISMIC SHIFT IN THE MARKETING LANDSCAPE

Already PR is gaining a bigger seat at the table. Consider this: in a recent study[1] by the University of Southern California Annenberg School for Communication, senior managers rated PR one of the top three contributors to organizational success. That's right, PR was right at the top, beating almost every other major corporate function, including sales, human resources, legal, strategic planning, information systems, and security. Just a few years ago, senior managers ranked PR near the bottom of these same corporate functions. PR has come a long way in a short amount of time.

Many forces are thrusting PR to a new level of importance. To begin with, there's *fragmentation*. Until recently, reaching your customers was relatively simple. Chances were they got their news and entertainment from watching prime-time television and reading the local newspaper—just like everybody else. To raise awareness about your product or service, all you had to do was develop a clever ad campaign and perhaps work to gain some positive press coverage.

Thanks to the Internet, people are now getting their news and entertainment from a wider variety of sources. Believe it or not, consumers are actually spending more time online than in front of their TVs. When surfing the Internet, consumers are choosing from literally thousands of sources for news and information. Today more than 160 million Web sites exist in cyberspace[2], with more sites being added every second.

In addition to creating a forum for consumer-generated media, the Internet has led the mainstream media to move online. Three out of ten Americans regularly go online to get their news.[3] To keep up, almost every prominent print publication has added an online counterpart, be it NYTimes.com, WSJ.com, or Salon.com. The Internet has also led to the creation of hundreds of new radio stations. Together, XM Satellite Radio and Sirius Satellite Radio offer more than 200 radio stations to a total of almost 18 million U.S. subscribers.[4] In addition, more than 1,200 radio stations are broadcasting with high-definition radio technology,[5] doubling or tripling the number of channels available to listeners. Similar trends are occurring worldwide.

Not only have print and radio become more *fragmented*, so too has television. Long gone are the days of three major television networks. The advent of satellite and cable television has given television audiences ten to twenty times as many channels from which to choose. What's more, an increasing number of television viewers are using cutting-edge technology to block out the ads. All of this means that reaching your customers has become a lot more complicated than it was five years, three years, or even one year ago.

The second trend is *saturation*. The marketing landscape has become increasingly crowded, making it harder than ever to cut through the advertising clutter. A growing number of companies are competing to promote their products and services, creating a marketing blitz like never before. The average American is exposed to 3,000 ads every day, far more information than is possible to absorb, making it more difficult than ever to establish strong awareness for any one product or service.

Third, there's *reputation*. The interactive atmosphere of the Internet has made it possible for information about your company to spread rapidly. Internet blogs and chat rooms have created popular forums for employees to expose the good, the bad, and the ugly about life within your four walls while giving consumers a strong voice about their experiences with the products and services they buy. Today companies are susceptible to public scrutiny from nearly every direction.

With an overabundance of products and services from which to choose, consumers are increasingly distinguishing companies by reputation, and they're using the Internet to learn the details. According to a recent national opinion survey, nearly 65 percent of people say it's important to buy from socially responsible companies, while 79 percent say it's important to work for one. Almost half of the survey respondents said they've used the Internet to learn about a company's reputation.[6]

PR, YOUR MOST STRATEGIC WEAPON

As *fragmentation, saturation,* and *reputation* become the catchwords of the day, traditional advertising is losing the luster it once had. For one thing, it's becoming more difficult to reach large numbers of consumers through advertising. In the fragmented and saturated landscape, ads have become less effective at breaking through all the noise.

Second, ads are a less cost-effective medium for building awareness. Think about this: When we recently helped one of our clients place a news article in the *Wall Street Journal*, the total cost was about $18,000 in PR labor. Placing an ad of the same size would have cost our client about $99,300 in advertising fees, more than five times as much.

Third, as companies seek to build their reputations, ads are seen as the less credible vehicle for doing so. Today's sophisticated audiences are quick to spot what they perceive as "spin." They want to know that the information they receive is from a credible source. Unlike an ad, which contains only your messages, a news article typically includes a wider range of perspectives, making it more believable. Which carries greater credibility, a three-minute news segment or a thirty-second commercial? And by the way, which is capable of offering up a more complex message? The fact that PR results in news stories that are written by objective third-party sources makes it the most credible discipline for shaping perceptions about a company, product, or service.

Many CEOs have begun to see PR as the prime contributor to organizational success and are backing this view with their wallets. At the same time that advertising budgets tighten, companies are starting to invest heavily in PR. Over the next five years, PR spending is expected to increase 11.8 percent to $4.26 billion, according to the 2007 *Veronis Suhler Stevenson Communications Industry Forecast*.[7] In addition, the U.S. Department of Labor reports that employment in the public relations field is expected to grow faster than average for all occupations through 2012. "The need for good public relations in an increasingly competitive business environment should spur demand for PR specialists in organizations of all types and sizes," the bureau said in its report. "And in the wake of corporate scandals, more emphasis will be placed on improving the image of the client, as well as building public confidence."[8]

TRAPPED IN THE TACTICAL

While companies are starting to understand the connection between PR and organizational success, most continue to approach it at the tactical level, failing to harness the full power this medium can provide. PR professionals generate one press release after the next without developing a comprehensive game plan for what they're trying to achieve. They become obsessed with press coverage without stopping to consider how the editorial coverage they garner furthers their company's business objectives. Senior executives often relegate PR to the marketing department, failing to build consensus for PR within the broader organization. They miss important opportunities to build PR into key business activities. They take a reactive approach to PR, abandoning the plan they have in place to accommodate random requests from high-level executives. And they flush thousands of dollars down the drain without stopping to measure their "bang for the buck."

What all this adds up to is bad results, and bad results mean lost credibility for both you and your company. The effects of a poor PR program can be devastating. The media and analyst communities stop paying attention. Employees don't see results and become discouraged. It becomes more difficult to attract top PR staff and agencies. Board members become increasingly reluctant to assign more budget. Executives don't see the power of PR and start giving it a bad name.

Sometimes companies remain trapped in the tactical because of lack of knowledge. We don't know what we don't know, especially when there's no one around to tell us. PR professionals quickly work their way up the ladder, learning the tactics of writing press releases and pitching stories to the media. Often, however, their training lacks instruction on how to view PR with a broader, more strategic lens. Similarly, company managers with other responsibilities suddenly find themselves in charge of PR, expected to know how and what to do without any real coaching. The truth is the number of mentors who really know how to use PR today are few and far between.

In other cases, companies get stuck in the tactical for lack of time. For a while now, we've had to face the reality that business is moving at an ever-faster clip. Most of us are being asked to revamp key operational functions to bring them in line with the new business reality while responding on a dime to an increasing number of executive and customer requests, not to speak of the growing volume of e-mail in our inboxes. The truth is that the hurried pace of business these days doesn't leave much time for strategic thinking.

Yet it's exactly this frantic pace that makes it vital to spend time thinking about your PR strategy. Because the current climate makes it so easy to get sidetracked, it's more critical than ever to develop a plan, understand that plan, and stay focused on it so that you don't go off on some tangent and never find your way back. It's true that developing a strategic PR program requires some time and thought. But the good news is that if it's done right, you can actually save money and preserve your company's limited resources by carrying out only those PR tactics that further your core business objectives.

A sound strategy will not only help you use your existing budget more wisely, we firmly believe companies that use their resources well are continually rewarded with more resources over time. It's like fishing for salmon in the ocean. If you harvest salmon responsibly, they'll eventually be replenished. But if you remove the salmon from the ocean all at once, the salmon will disappear. In the same way, if you use your PR resources strategically, you'll get great results, which leads to larger budgets, whether from your venture capital firm or your board of directors. But if you squander your resources on tactical measures that don't add up, eventually your PR budget will dry up.

A STRATEGIC ROAD MAP FOR SUCCESS

Unlike most other books on the market that focus on developing press releases and other PR tactics, *Strategic Public Relations* connects the dots to show you how you can use PR strategically to accomplish your company's most important business objectives. By reading this book, you won't learn how to write a press release or pitch a bylined article to the media. Plenty of introductory PR books that handle these subjects effectively are already on the market. Instead, *Strategic Public Relations* provides a high-level road map to help you use PR more strategically to boost your company's market share and increase your business success.

The first pages of the book explain why a strategic approach to PR is critical to your success. Specifically, you'll learn what PR can do and what it can't. You'll also learn why harnessing your PR program to your broader business strategy is your golden key to success. The book then provides ten guiding principles designed to help you take your PR program to a more strategic level. Most of these principles are straightforward and simple; none involves rocket science. Yet it's important to take the time to think about how you can apply these principles to your business and then make a wholehearted effort to implement them continually.

The guiding principles offered in this book and the real-life lessons that accompany them are based on a tried-and-true approach to PR that we have developed and perfected over the course of our careers. Over the last decade and a half, we have had the privilege to work on the inside of worldwide PR agencies such as Waggener Edstrom and within the walls of influential corporations such as Microsoft, RealNetworks, AT&T Wireless, and Tegic Communications/AOL. We've worked in the trenches with small and medium-size businesses and major corporations in a variety of industries, helping them to develop thoughtful PR programs that accrue to their larger company story. Most recently, we've established our own PR firm, Communiqué PR, which provides strategic counsel and tactical execution to help cutting-edge companies achieve their toughest business objectives.

MAKING PR COME ALIVE

Our experience over the last two decades has taught us firsthand what makes PR blossom and what makes it wither on the vine. We've experienced the frustration of watching businesses discount the value of PR because they don't know how to use it strategically. We've also watched the extraordinary breakthroughs that occur when companies leverage PR to its fullest potential.

The inspiration for writing this book comes from our cumulative experience and from our passion for helping companies use PR to achieve maximum results. Have you ever watched a colleague struggle to convey an important point but fail to find the words to do it effectively? In the same way, many companies have a compelling story to tell but lack the know-how to communicate their message with impact. By writing this book, our goal is to help you achieve maximum results by telling your story in the most meaningful and powerful way.

In addition to our own insights, *Strategic Public Relations* contains firsthand behind-the-scenes stories from today's foremost PR experts. You'll see what's worked and what hasn't through the eyes of PR practitioners at companies such as Nike, Starbucks, Deloitte, Seattle Children's Hospital, Cranium, Alaska Airlines, Linden Lab, Big Fish Games, and Knowledge Anywhere. The book also contains shrewd lessons from influential journalists and analysts as well as anecdotes from many other well-known companies such as Procter & Gamble, Harley-Davidson, McDonald's, Google, General Motors, Apple, Home Depot, Blockbuster, and Coca-Cola.

If you want to learn how to navigate the new communications landscape, if you want to discover how to use PR more strategically, if you want to understand how to get top results for every PR dollar you spend, this book is for you. In short, *Strategic Public Relations* is for anyone who wants to use PR to its fullest potential.

Michael Dell, the founder and CEO of Dell, once said, "It's through curiosity and looking at opportunities in new ways that we've always mapped our path at Dell . . . There's always an opportunity to make a difference."[9] We hope *Strategic Public Relations* opens up the opportunities your company needs to propel it toward maximum success.

THE CASE FOR A STRATEGIC APPROACH TO PR

S ay you work for a confectionery company that produces chewing gum. Sales of your leading chewing gum have been flat in recent months, and company executives aren't sure what to do. After talking to your colleagues, you decide to launch a public relations program. The goal is to boost awareness of your gum by issuing at least one press release each week and distributing it broadly. Whether there's real news to announce or not, you methodically put out a press release every week—an announcement about a new retail chain that's carrying your chewing gum, an endorsement from a small-time sponsor, a new hire in your company—anything to keep your gum top of mind in the media.

At first your efforts seem to be working. Your press releases lead to a few small mentions here and there, usually in the business brief section of newspapers. But it's now been fifteen weeks since you launched the PR program, and coverage has started to drop off. Even worse, *BusinessWeek* just ran a full-length, positive story about your competitor's initiative to test new stress-reducing and teeth-whitening varieties of gum. Your company wasn't even mentioned, and the board of directors wants to know why. In a panic, you call *BusinessWeek* to pitch a story about your company. It's too late, you're told. *BusinessWeek* readers will find only so many chewing gum stories compelling.

On the face of it, it seems that your efforts ought to work. The idea is to raise visibility of your chewing gum so more consumers will buy it. Yet the approach is fundamentally flawed. Why? *Because your PR program isn't tied to your company's broader business strategy.* To be successful, your company needs to better understand its business objectives and then make sure all of its PR efforts map back to these goals. What are the sales goals of your confectionery company over the next year, and which customers are you intending to reach? Why have sales slipped in recent months? How do consumers view your company?

Is the market for chewing gum growing or shrinking? How are your competitors positioning themselves? What makes your chewing gum different? What are the perceived strengths and weaknesses of your business? Issuing a stream of press releases without knowing the answers to these questions is a complete waste of time. Likewise, competing for the most coverage without a targeted plan for the exact type of coverage you're seeking flushes your precious resources down the drain. It's a tactical approach to PR that generates little to no results.

Increasingly organizations are viewing PR as a key strategy to business success. Indeed, PR spending is expected to grow by almost 12 percent to $4.26 billion in the next four years, according to Veronis Suhler Stevenson, a New York investment firm that specializes in media.[1] But while companies are spending more money on PR, the majority of today's organizations continue to engage PR at the tactical level. They opt for instant gratification, striving to obtain coverage—any coverage, as long as it's positive—for the sake of greater visibility. And they try to beat their competitors at the coverage game, as if there's a direct relationship between news stories and sales, without mapping their PR goals back to their overall business objectives. Some may succeed in attracting news coverage. But without a targeted approach, they are failing to reap the stellar results that PR is capable of delivering. As Michael Levine writes in his book, *Guerilla P.R.,* "The notion that P.R. is simply a matter of mailing press releases is nuttier than a squirrel's breakfast."[2]

A STRATEGIC APPROACH TO PR

PR is a powerful tool that can help companies accomplish everything from building their brands to increasing demand for their products to boosting employee morale. To obtain these benefits, however, organizations must learn to use PR far more strategically than most are doing today. Says author and military strategist Sun Tzu, "The general who wins a battle makes many calculations in his temple ere the battle is fought. The general who loses a battle makes but few calculations beforehand."[3] In the same way, to reap the full business value PR has to offer, businesses must work harder upfront to identify their strategy. They should refrain from jumping directly to the execution phase and should instead spend some time calculating exactly what they want to achieve.

Creating a PR program is similar to building a house. Before you begin, you need a blueprint that maps out the design and layout of the house. There's no sense figuring out whether you want a glass door or a wood door without first deciding what your overall floor plan is going to look like and how you will use the space. Likewise, writing a press release, holding a press conference, launching a company Web site, or pitching a story to the media are useless efforts without your first mapping out the way these efforts tie into your broader business strategy. By jumping straight into PR tactics, companies end up engaging in a series of isolated efforts that don't contribute to the larger goal. As a result, they end up spinning their wheels and wasting their precious resources on efforts that do little to move their business forward. Gaining visibility without a clear understanding of what form that increased visibility should take leaves companies trapped in the tactical. A strategic approach, on the other hand, means having a clear understanding of the direction in which you want your business to head and then using PR to help get you there.

"I think a strategic approach involves really planning in advance to determine what audience you want to target and what messages you want to relate to that audience," says Jennifer Seymour, director of public relations for Seattle Children's Hospital. For Seattle Children's Hospital, the approach includes pitching health education and human interest stories to the local and regional media to build awareness of the hospital among potential patients as well as the general community. It also involves promoting the hospital's research nationally to attract doctors, researchers, and nurses. "PR is an important tool to help people in our industry understand what we're doing, and to demonstrate that we're conducting cutting-edge research," Seymour says. "It's also something we use to educate people about the hospital in a way that builds our donor population and helps us attract new employees."

So where do you start? To take a strategic approach to PR, you must first *clearly define your top business objectives.* What does your company want to achieve, and how? Once you've defined this, it suddenly becomes clear what audiences you should target and what PR tools you should use to help accomplish these goals. Here is a full list of questions you should answer to help you identify your organization's business objectives and what you want PR to help you achieve:

- How do we generate revenue?
- Who are our most important customers?
- Who are the business decision-makers for our products or services?
- Who are our target audiences?
- What are their current perceptions of our company?
- Who are our biggest competitors?
- How are our competitors positioning themselves?
- How do we differentiate our products or services from those of our competitors?
- What is our value proposition, and is it well understood?
- How do we think the competitive landscape is going to shift?

- What are the category dynamics? Is the category growing or shrinking?
- What are our top business objectives in the next six months? The next year? Three years?
- What are our mission and vision? What do we do today, and where are we going?
- What are the biggest opportunities and challenges for our business?
- What are the perceived strengths and weaknesses of the business?
- What are the implications for communications as we move forward?

Answering these questions may seem like a lot of work. Unfortunately, however, there are no shortcuts. Lack of a strategic framework will only lead to inefficiency and missed opportunities. It's essential that you think through the answers to these questions before embarking on any PR campaign.

A FOCUSED APPROACH

Once you've defined your business direction, being strategic means *focusing your PR program only on those efforts that help you move the business forward*. For example, perhaps one of the obstacles the confectionery company faces is that its chewing gum hasn't gotten much traction in the adult market because it's not seen as healthy or beneficial by the millions of adults seeking to lose weight. If your goal is to get more overweight adults to buy your gum, one approach might be to position your CEO as a thought leader in weight management. To do this, you may want to line up speaking opportunities at weight loss conferences and place bylined articles authored by your CEO in the most popular health and dieting magazines.

Or perhaps you've found that your chewing gum isn't popular among school-age children. To increase demand for your gum among kids, you may want to promote games on your Web site via children's publications. Or you might want to run a series of articles convincing parents of the health benefits of chewing gum after meals. Note that suddenly it becomes irrelevant if your competitor gets an article placed in *Business Week*. If parents primarily read *Parenting Magazine*, getting an article placed in *Business Week* doesn't drive you toward your goal.

A Focused Approach to PR: How PR Helped Tegic Raise Its Sales Value

In the fall of 1997, the Seattle-based firm Tegic Communications was ready to market its innovative new product that made text input more efficient on mobile phones. Called T9, the technology enabled users to type in messages much faster and with far fewer keystrokes than had been possible previously.

Tegic wanted to use PR to achieve its business objective of getting its T9 technology included as a standard feature in every mobile phone on the market. "We chose PR over other marketing tools because we felt it would buy us more credibility and more reach for the dollar," says Don Davidge, the company's former vice president of marketing and sales. "We really had validation from the CEO at the top all the way down that PR was critically important."

From the beginning, Tegic executives realized two things about their T9 technology. First, it wasn't realistic to think it would attract stand-alone coverage. Because T9 was a feature that mobile phone handset manufacturers could decide to include in their phones, more likely it would be mentioned in mobile phone buying guides or in stories discussing the growth of text messaging. Second, people had to see the technology firsthand to get excited about it. If you described it to them by phone, they didn't understand its significance. But if you demonstrated to them in person, it was as if a lightbulb went off.

As a result, the PR team worked to draw a large volume of press coverage by securing mentions of T9 in stories written about wireless handsets. The company issued a press release every time a new mobile handset manufacturer licensed its T9 technology. It also worked to secure third-party referrals from wireless carriers and handset manufacturers about the benefit of T9 on handsets.

In addition, Tegic trained about half of its staff to demonstrate the T9 technology to the media as they traveled around the world for other meetings. "We were a little company with a tight budget based in Seattle, while most of the market was in Europe and Asia," Davidge says. "By training so many people to serve as spokespeople for Tegic, we were able to greatly extend our reach."

Awareness of Tegic and T9 soon grew exponentially, leading the company to begin developing a new instant messaging product. At the time, AOL and Microsoft were engaged in a major battle over the instant messaging market, and the media was covering it closely.

Although its new product was still in the development stage, Tegic decided to take advantage of all the media interest in instant messaging by announcing its product in advance. It was a controversial move, but it quickly paid off. AOL took notice and ended up buying Tegic four months later in December 1999.

"We sold the company for $350 million, which was a huge success for us," Davidge says. "Afterward an AOL executive told me his team had internally calculated they paid an extra $50 million for Tegic just because of how much buzz there was about the company. $50 million in two years—now that's the power of PR."

Being strategic also means *taking a long runway approach to PR.* Sometimes the marketplace changes or a crisis unexpectedly happens, and you have to change gears and respond quickly. Yet often executives become too focused on what their competitors are doing or react to the latest trend and lose sight of the big picture. Constantly changing direction can quickly derail your PR campaign by preventing you from obtaining the momentum needed for success. It's the same kind of disaster that can happen by starting your plane down the runway only to abort the takeoff. To get results, you need to be consistent and let the momentum build. Taking a long runway approach to PR means driving toward your long-term goals rather than constantly responding to the immediate environment.

"Strategic PR is a marathon rather than a sprint," says Anthony Bay, chairman of MOD Systems, a Seattle-based digital media company. "It's not enough to simply craft a few polished messages. You need to have a compelling story, and you have to make sure the messages you develop truly map to what the media finds of interest. You need to be a consistent and reliable source of information not just about your company but about the industry and market. You need to be personable and engaging while remaining honest and not offended by challenging questions. All of this takes time and persistence, but if done right, it eventually pays off."

KNOWING WHEN TO USE PR

To get the most out of PR, you also need to know what PR can help you accomplish and what it can't. A question many of our clients ask is when they should use PR as opposed to advertising. Both play a significant role in the marketing mix; the trick is to know when to use each.

While companies are starting to invest more heavily in PR, they are still spending a much larger chunk of their marketing budgets on advertising. The $4.5 billion U.S. organizations spend annually on PR is just a drop in the bucket compared to the total $775 billion spent on overall marketing communications.[4] Spending a lot of money on ads made sense during a time when most people watched prime-time television and read their local newspaper. But with fewer people watching TV and the circulation of many newspapers and magazines declining, advertising is becoming a less effective medium.

The media landscape is becoming far more fragmented than it once was, with people getting their news and information from a much broader range of sources. As a result, it's becoming increasingly difficult to reach large numbers of consumers through advertising. As Al and Laura Ries write in their book *The Fall of Advertising and the Rise of PR,* "Yesterday it was advertising. Today it's PR . . . In the future clients will be looking to public relations firms to help them set the strategic directions for brands, and advertising will be forced to follow the lead of PR."[5]

The big advantage of advertising is that it gives companies total control over the message. You can place an ad in any publication you want, completely scripting the message and when and how often it is seen. With PR you don't have that same level of control. Each time you pitch a story to the media, a reporter runs it through his or her own objective filter. The story will likely include quotes from other sources. You don't know when the media outlet will run the story, and you can't be sure the story will be positive or negative. A major advantage of PR, however, is that it offers more credibility than advertising. Everyone knows ads are bought and paid for, which makes them less believable. By contrast, when a story about your company appears in an independent publication, it carries a great deal of credibility. Reading the article, customers get a balanced story and believe they are drawing their own conclusions about your company and your product.

"If a CEO told you how good his company is, you'd think he was bragging," says Bay, the MOD Systems chairman. "But if a customer told you the same thing, you're more likely to believe it. Why? Because the customer is less biased and is speaking from personal experience. The same comparison holds true for PR versus advertising. With PR, a third-party news organization or industry analyst tells people about your company. A PR placement can be more believable than an ad or paid endorsement because it reflects an unbiased position."

Another advantage of PR over advertising is its ability to educate. Whereas advertising entertains with images, PR tells stories with words. It's hard to deliver a complex message with a fifteen- to thirty-second TV commercial, yet an article placed in a publication offers just that opportunity. It has the ability to educate customers about complex products and services, describing in detail what makes them beneficial. In general, the more complicated the story you want to tell and the more innovative or creative your product, the more important PR becomes. In today's technology-driven economy, where the success of products increasingly rests on their innovation and creativity, PR is usually the best vehicle for raising awareness about your products and services.

Finally, PR is often more cost-effective than advertising. The cost of developing and running ads can be prohibitive, especially for small companies. PR campaigns can usually be carried out at a fraction of the cost, often with a better return on investment. Indeed, a recent study by Procter & Gamble, the worldwide consumer products group, found that the return from PR campaigns is often better than from traditional forms of advertising. As Anthony Rose, associate director for global beauty external relations at Procter & Gamble, told the *Advertiser*, "Public relations has come a long way as a marketing tool in the past few years . . . PR plays a key role here by offering up relevant and credible information directly and indirectly through influencers. Also, it's often more cost efficient and offers maximum return on investment."[6]

A Strategic Approach to PR

What's the difference between a tactical and a strategic approach to public relations? We asked this question to PR professionals at a wide variety of organizations. The following is a representative sampling of their responses.

"A strategic approach to PR is an approach that answers the question, 'What are the company's goals, and how can PR support the company achieving its goals?' By contrast, a tactical approach simply doesn't address that question. I've seen lots of companies just blast information out onto the wire and even go on press tours without really thinking through the impression they want to make, or why. That's only marginally useful."
—**Rick Romatowski,** former chief operating officer, Open Interface

"To me, a strategic approach involves picking a point of view around a campaign versus just looking for publicity. First and foremost, it involves understanding the business objectives of the company and business unit you're supporting. It's having an intimate knowledge of the competitive landscape as well as the audiences you're trying to reach. And once you understand all that, you develop your messaging and a set of measurements for success."
—**Keith Lindenburg**, director, national public relations, Deloitte Services LP

"If you're thinking tactically, you're trying to build instant revenues. PR is something that has to build over time. Through PR, you start to establish repeated exposure to your brand, and over time people begin to see you as a trusted company."
—**Paul Thelen**, founder, Big Fish Games

"Being strategic means knowing what kind of story you want to tell and where to place it. It also means getting your messages across in a memorable way."
—**Richard Tait**, founder, Cranium

"I think it takes some deep thinking to do public relations properly. It all starts with the company's mission and vision. It's important to think of your company as a brand, and make sure the brand informs all of your public relations efforts. It's also important to be focused. You don't want to be everywhere. You have a lot more influence if you're in the right place at the right time with the right story."
—**Lee Weinstein**, former director of global communications, Nike

"I think the main difference is where the PR strategy resides in the food chain. A lot of times people make PR an afterthought as opposed to an integral part of the whole plan. They have their pricing and distribution, their promotional strategy—all the components of the traditional marketing mix—and then they say, 'Oh, let's get some PR for that also.' They view PR simply as a way to generate awareness, but the question is, 'Awareness for what purpose? What is it you want PR to deliver for the company?'"
—**Brad Stevens**, former vice president of U.S. marketing, Starbucks

As a general rule of thumb, PR is the best tool for introducing a new product or service, expanding your customer base, or shifting public perceptions. Advertising, on the other hand, is the most effective tool for reinforcing a brand once it becomes well-known and the opportunities for publicity start to dwindle. As Al Ries told brandchannel.com, "Advertising is something like cheerleading. You reinforce ideas that are already there. Our message is that after a while there is no publicity potential in a new brand. People wrote up Red Bull, but today? Now they have to shift to advertising to maintain the brand. Same thing with powerful brands like Coca-Cola. You're just not going to get much publicity."[7]

WHAT PR CAN ACCOMPLISH

Public relations is all about shaping public perception. The goal of any public relations campaign is to solidify or shift how something is viewed, whether it is a product, service, concept, or company. If used strategically, PR can help improve almost every aspect of a business. Following are some examples of the ways in which PR can help you achieve your most important business objectives:

- *Build your brand.* PR can help you build your brand by validating the innovation of your products and services. For example, when Knowledge Anywhere began developing custom e-learning solutions for businesses in 1998, very few companies even knew what e-learning was. This meant that Knowledge Anywhere had to develop awareness about itself, its products, and the entire e-learning industry simultaneously. To do this, the company bypassed advertising altogether, turning instead to PR, which gave it more room to introduce and explain the meaning and significance of e-learning. "If we had run a full-page ad saying we're Knowledge Anywhere, a custom developer of online learning solutions, people would have simply flipped to the next page thinking, 'I don't know what they're talking about,'" says Bill Strelke, the company's former executive vice president of marketing and business development. "So instead, we authored our own articles, got into the local newspaper and spoke at industry trade shows. PR played a huge role early on helping us to develop awareness for our company as well as the products we were promoting."

- *Increase demand for your product or service.* PR can help articulate the benefits of your product or service by explaining in detail why other customers purchased it, how they used it, and what problems it helped them solve. By reading a case study about how a similar customer purchased accounting software, for example, other customers can determine whether the software will be useful to them. PR can also increase demand by providing information that consumers can use to compare products and services. For example, Giant Campus, which offers summer technology camps at colleges throughout the United States, provides a series of tips for choosing the right computer summer camp on its Web site. By offering these tips, the company provides useful information to parents about how to select a camp while also indirectly making a case for the thinking behind its own summer camps.

- *Broaden your customer base.* PR is a great tool for helping you expand the appeal of your product or service to new customer segments. For example, financial software maker Intuit recently used PR in an innovative way to reach potential young customers. The company generated widespread editorial coverage around a TurboTax Tax Rap contest on YouTube in which it agreed to pay $25,000 to the person who created the best rap video featuring TurboTax. The contest, which was judged by rapper Vanilla Ice, drew more than 370 video entries, all of which were featured on a special-purpose Web site that Intuit built on a YouTube page. Intuit publicized the contest and winners through blogs, newspaper articles, and industry trade publications. In the end, the rap videos were viewed more than 2.5 million times, introducing the TurboTax brand to a whole new generation of taxpayers.[8]

  Another example of a company using PR to reach out to a new customer segment is U.S. motorcycle manufacturer Harley-Davidson. The company, whose traditional white male client base is aging, recently decided to use public relations to convince women to ride Harleys. Harley-Davidson added a section to its Web site featuring women and motorcycling, complete with a history of women motorcycle riders, a featured Harley women rider of the month, and information about learning to ride. As part of the campaign, Harley also hosted garage parties for women across the United States, similar to Tupperware parties that brought women together in the past. In part due to these efforts, 10 percent of all the motorcycles Harley sells each year are now bought by women. "The presence of freedom, empowerment and exhilaration are universally appealing," Paul James, communications manager for Harley-Davidson, told *Road & Travel Magazine.* "More and more women are recognizing that fact, which is one reason why this is a growing trend in motorcycling."[9]

- *Create trust for your company and its products.* Because PR is viewed as more credible than advertising, it's a great tool for helping customers understand that they can trust your product. For example, Big Fish Games, a developer of casual, downloadable games, has used PR to steadily build credibility for its games among investors, game developers, media, and consumers. This strategy has helped Big Fish quickly earn a place at the table along with RealNetworks, Microsoft, and Yahoo. The company, which was started in 2002, is now the world's largest game distribution portal, delivering more than 1 million downloads daily. "It's a very big hurdle for someone to pull out a credit card and submit it to a site they don't know, so establishing Big Fish Games as a trusted company was very important long-term," says Paul Thelen, the company's founder and chief strategy officer. "That doesn't happen with a single press release. That happens when people see our products at various retail stores, and read about us in articles written about the industry. Through PR, we started to establish repeated exposure to our brand, and that cemented in people's minds that we're a legitimate company."

- *Establish a leadership position for your company.* PR can propel your company to a leadership position by positioning it as a leader in your category. For example, Starbucks, which spent less than $10 million on advertising in its first ten years,[10] established itself as a leading coffee retailer using a powerful PR program. Even today, PR plays a key role for Starbucks in generating awareness in addition to in-store promotions. Starbucks has accomplished this by developing a unique concept and then using PR to tell its story, which is about quality, passion, innovation, and customer loyalty. It also has launched a series of PR-driven campaigns centered on themes such as fair-trade coffee and clean water, helping to enhance its reputation as a good corporate citizen.

  With the help of PR, Starbucks has been able to position itself as a unique new force that signals the rebirth of coffee culture in America, according to Brad Stevens, former vice president of U.S. marketing at Starbucks. "What PR brought us was third-party credibility," Stevens says. "We weren't saying how great we were. There were others that were saying how great we were. PR allowed us to connect with customers on more of a grassroots level. It was almost like customers were discovering something new that a trusted source was telling them about versus Starbucks advertising and trying to convince a customer that what we were doing was special and different."

- *Shift the perception of your product.* PR is also a useful tool for changing the way customers view your product. For example, The Piaggio Group, maker of Vespa motor scooters, used PR to shift the perception of its scooters as a fashionable recreational vehicle to a viable transportation alternative in the midst of rising gasoline prices and growing concerns about energy use. To do this, the company used a multifaceted approach. It ran an open letter in the *New York Times* urging the mayors of U.S. cities to reduce their oil consumption by making their cities more scooter-friendly. It pitched a series of stories to transportation and consumer publications and took reporters on tandem Vespa rides so they could experience the scooters firsthand. It also developed customized podcasts highlighting the economic and environmental benefits of owning a scooter. Since the campaign was launched in June 2005, sales of Vespa scooters have increased by more than 25 percent.[11]

- *Develop awareness of a new product or service.* Because the messages required to convince customers to buy have become more complex, PR is often the best tool for building awareness of a new product or service. For example, McDonald's relied heavily on PR when it launched its premium salad line in the wake of childhood obesity claims. The strategy helped McDonald's regain momentum at a time when criticism was mounting from burger-bashing documentaries such as *Super Size Me*. At the same time that it introduced premium salads, McDonald's hired Bob Greene, Oprah Winfrey's personal trainer, to launch a new "balanced, active lifestyles" campaign. The campaign generated huge media interest, drew 5.7 million hits to its www.goactive.com Web site, and increased store traffic by 2.3 million U.S. customers per day. "That was one of those magical PR programs that did everything," Al Golin, chairman of McDonald's PR agency, GolinHarris, told *PRWeek*. "It set the cornerstone for a whole new attitude at McDonald's."[12]

- *Strengthen employee morale and attract first-rate talent to your company.* Employees like to work for companies that are credible and trustworthy, maintain momentum, and are making meaningful contributions to the broader world. Every time an employee sees her CEO interviewed in a news story about the industry, it makes her believe she's chosen the right company to work for. Likewise, each time people read about a company that treats its employees well and encourages them to make significant contributions to the greater world, it increases the company's reputation as a desirable place to work. Take Patagonia, an outdoor apparel company in Ventura, California, for example. Patagonia pledges at least 1 percent of gross sales to the protection and restoration of the natural environment. Employees can leave the company for up to two months to work for environmental organizations of their choice. Since its beginning, Patagonia has used PR to build awareness of the company culture, developing a reputation as a socially responsible company and a great place to work. The company has been cited again and again among the top companies for which to work and has been written up numerous times for its innovative products and progressive work environment. The company receives an average of 200 resumes a month,[13] with employee turnover in the single digits, according to the Patagonia Web site.[14]

- *Enhance the perceived value of your company.* When it comes time to sell your business, PR provides the opportunity to increase the perceived value of your company. For example, public relations played an essential role in setting the stage for the $350 million sale of Tegic Communications to AOL in 1999.[15] One of the things we did was to help the entire company understand Tegic's business objectives and the role PR would play in helping us to get there. Once a month, Tegic's department heads met with employees as a group to discuss where the company was headed and to obtain their feedback. For example, the vice president of sales updated employees about new licensing agreements that were signed while we in the marketing department discussed our PR strategy. Employees were very enthusiastic about the coverage we were garnering and understood how it supported the big picture. By cultivating a culture of communication, Tegic was able to establish a shared vision and motivate employees to grow the business, and this ultimately helped increase the monetary value of the company at the time of the acquisition.

- *Establish your company as socially responsible.* Many CEOs consider enhancing corporate reputation as the most important role that public relations can play. According to a joint survey by *PRWeek* and the PR firm Burson-Marsteller, more than 90 percent of CEOs say communication is "very important" or "important" for managing reputation, safeguarding the company's image, and crisis management.[16]

   Susan Johnston, vice president of public relations for Clearwire Corporation, a wireless broadband provider based in Kirkland, Washington, has spent the past two decades helping companies establish reputations as good corporate citizens. At Nextel Partners, for example, her company provided cell phones and free service to support local organizations that resonated with the community.

And at McCaw Cellular, which later became AT&T Wireless Services, her company sponsored community activities such as an annual July Fourth fireworks celebration and a community art project in which Seattle residents created parts of the American flag, illustrating what America means to them. Projects like these create the opportunity for employees to participate in their community while extending an organization's visibility. "All things being equal, most people like to buy from companies that are reputable, have a stake in the community, and are giving something back," Johnston says.

WHEN TO ENGAGE PR
So at what point in your company's growth should you engage PR? Should you do so right from the start or wait until you're earning a certain amount of revenue? The answer is *it depends*. In some cases, you may want to lay low for a while and fly below the radar without drawing attention from the competition—say, for example, if you've just started out and are still honing your product or service. In some cases, growth will occur naturally, and PR isn't necessary, for instance, if you're a consultancy and you're already growing at the desired pace without much marketing. But in other cases, it makes sense to attract publicity right out of the gate rather than waiting until later, for example, if you own a private bus company that needs to attract full busloads from day one to be profitable. In general, to evaluate whether the time is right for a PR program, consider how quickly you want your company to grow and whether you need PR to help you get there.

HOW TO APPROACH THIS BOOK
Each of the ten principles that follows is designed to help you approach PR more strategically. The principles show you how to sell PR to key stakeholders within your company, select a winning PR team, identify your target audiences, leverage emerging technologies, develop a strategic PR plan, craft a compelling story, build strategic relationships with the media, maintain an open information flow as you roll out the plan, measure and merchandise your results, and keep your PR program relevant over time. To help you fully understand each principle, each chapter is accompanied by real-life stories from companies that have put these principles into practice.

All the chapters in *Strategic Public Relations* are written to be fully comprehensible on their own; you can skip among chapters based on the specific needs and interests of your organization. To get the most out of this book, however, we recommend you read it sequentially because each principle builds on the one before it. Ultimately, the value you derive from the book depends on how well you put these principles to work for your organization. To that end, we recommend you revisit the book from time to time to make sure you're on the right track. Regardless of your position in your organization or PR agency, *Strategic Public Relations* shows you how to obtain top PR results for your business. Our hope is that by reading the ten principles that follow and turning them into reality, you'll begin to harness the full power PR has to offer.

SELL PR TO KEY STAKEHOLDERS WITHIN YOUR COMPANY

With PR, as with most things in life, it's impossible to focus your energy everywhere. A strategic approach to PR means concentrating your efforts only on those areas that support your most important business goals, and building consensus for PR right from the start ensures that everyone will rally behind the specific plan you end up implementing later down the line.

As you consider leveraging PR to help you accomplish your goals, it's critical that you gather support among key stakeholders in the organization. This means building support for PR as a strategic tool, some of the major PR activities you plan to implement, and the level of resources your organization is willing to spend on PR. By building consensus at the beginning, you eliminate the shots across the bow that will otherwise occur once you've developed your PR plan and have begun rolling it out. You also ensure that the specific plan you develop is in line with your organization's resources.

If key stakeholders in your organization haven't bought into PR, you can expect them to raise questions later during the process. They may not understand why PR is a priority. Or they may not have bought into the importance of the particular program you develop, failing to understand how it will bring about the company's business objectives. Suddenly you'll be operating in fire drill mode, wasting precious energy responding to people's complaints rather than proactively implementing your program to achieve the results you seek for your company.

THE IMPORTANCE OF BEING IN SYNC

Obtaining buy-in for your PR program from key stakeholders in your organization will ensure that everyone supports PR and the approach you've chosen. This step is critical because it will help you ascertain whether people are in agreement with the high-level objectives of the company and support your PR program to achieve those objectives. If people have differing opinions about the value of PR or the company's goals, it will quickly become evident, providing the opportunity for dialogue and the ability to align everyone in a single direction.

"It really starts from the outset with understanding the senior executives' objectives, and then communicating how PR can help," says Rick Romatowski, former chief operating officer at Open Interface North America, a pioneer in Bluetooth technology. "When you build consensus around what your goals are and then wrap that into your PR message, you know that everyone from the executives down to the salespeople will be offering up the same message."

Charlie Gillette, president and chief sales executive for Knowledge Anywhere, agrees. "I think the key is to explain at a high level how public relations will help the company achieve its business objectives and then gain consensus by bringing that to the board," he says. "When we did this at Knowledge Anywhere, there would be a few questions as to why we were doing this and what we were really after. But as long as we knew where we were going, what our goals were and the results we were after, board members would quickly fall into place and say, 'OK, I get it. I support that.'"

EMBRACING THE BEST IDEAS

Another reason that building consensus is important is that it provides the opportunity to obtain additional ideas and understand objections that may not have occurred to you. When you solicit others' opinions, you obtain new ideas, data points, and perspectives that lead to a better PR program. By failing to build consensus, you risk missing opportunities to leverage the power of PR and how to best leverage it. Think of the political genius of Abraham Lincoln and his effectiveness at bringing together his rivals to create his cabinet after he won the presidency. In her book *Team of Rivals*, Doris Kearns Goodwin documents how Lincoln, by embracing a wide range of opinions, was able to develop a course of action that ultimately allowed him to preserve the Union and win the Civil War.[1]

Similarly, PR managers can make wiser decisions by asking executives, the board of directors, and other key stakeholders to scrutinize their PR program. To develop the best course of action, they need to surround themselves with people who don't always agree with them, listen to them carefully, and incorporate the best ideas into their program.

Building consensus for PR helps you develop lasting relationships with key stakeholders within the organization. It helps make them feel included and empowered and that their opinion is valued. Conversely, failing to obtain buy-in can quickly lead to bruised egos. People may think you purposely kept them out of the loop, or they may get fired up, believing that you're not doing what they think needs to be done. Ultimately, they may fail to understand the value of PR and cut your budget in favor of other organizational priorities.

In *Getting to Yes*, authors Roger Fisher, William Ury, and Bruce Patton discuss how critical it is to allow others to participate in the process. "If they are not involved in the process, they are hardly likely to approve the product. It is that simple," they write. "If you want the other side to accept a disagreeable conclusion, it is crucial that you involve them in the process of reaching that conclusion."[2]

SHARING RESPONSIBILITY FOR SUCCESS

By building consensus for your PR program ahead of time, you also make sure that all key decision-makers share responsibility for success. The success of the program doesn't fall solely on your shoulders; it's shared by the team as a whole. In the same way that the head coach is ultimately responsible for the success of the football team but relies on the offensive and defensive coordinators to call the individual plays, the CEO is ultimately responsible for the success of the organization but looks to the PR manager to recommend the best approach. Obtaining buy-in all the way up to the CEO level empowers the CEO to keep the board and investors informed about why the approach you've chosen makes sense. It also allows you to go back later and say, "We all agreed that this was the right approach. It wasn't just me out there making the call."

When you fail to obtain buy-in, the consequences can be devastating. For example, a PR professional who worked for one of our clients had great ideas but failed to build consensus for his program. Eventually he was let go because the company wanted a team player who was willing to solicit other people's opinions and help the CEO keep stakeholders informed. Failing to share the PR strategy can put the CEO at risk with the board of directors, investors, and other company stakeholders.

By failing to assure collective agreement on your approach, you also run the risk that key stakeholders may undermine the company's goals. When PR managers fail to build consensus for their program, company stakeholders are more likely to move in different directions, offering the media information to advance their own agenda rather than that of the company as a whole.

Keys to a Successful Negotiation

Interview with Bruce Patton, cofounder of the Harvard Negotiation Project and coauthor of the best-selling book Getting to Yes.

Q: Why is it important to build consensus for your PR program before rolling it out?

Bruce Patton: If you don't have buy-in or agreement, people won't be very enthusiastic, and their behavior won't be consistent with your goals. Everything everyone does sends a message, and the message gets diluted or muddied when it's not consistent. It's important to point out that while consensus is a great goal, it doesn't necessarily imply unanimity. You don't have to get everybody on board and give everyone a veto. A better definition of consensus is having enough agreement to make it worthwhile to move ahead.

Q: What constitutes enough agreement to move ahead?

Patton: It's not a formula. It depends on the circumstances. The question is do enough key stakeholders support this to have a realistic chance of being successful?

Q: How should you handle the people who don't agree with your approach?

Patton: Beyond obtaining as much agreement as you can, there should be a second goal of making sure people who don't fully agree with your approach at least understand its rationale, validity, and integrity. If you can convey this, people's behavior will be much better. It's entirely possible to effectively support a decision you would make differently, but only if you understand the integrity of that decision.

Q: How can you make sure you convey the rationale of your approach?

Patton: It's important to have a dialogue. Don't just tell people what you think makes sense, and don't just ask them what to do, because that just forces them to take a position. Ask them what issues or needs they think ought to be addressed, and make sure they feel you hear them. Ask them what they feel is important and how they would rank one interest against another so you understand all of their interests and the rationale and logic that lie beneath them. If you disagree, share what's valid about the person's perspective and where and why you differ. In general, don't just explain your solution, but also how you got there. Then ask people for their reaction. If they see things differently, try to figure out why. Seek to understand what you may be overlooking.

Q: Why do business people so often avoid building consensus?

Patton: There is a strong tendency to believe that the way we see the world is the way it really is. We have a built-in lack of humility that there could be things we're missing. It's a mark of a competent person to understand there are often multiple ways of looking at a situation and that each might have integrity. There's a lot of ambiguity out there, and there may be more than one path that leads to success. It can also be profoundly unsettling to have doubt about whether we've got the right answer. Often, we want to feel certain there aren't valid objections and that there's no chance of making a mistake, and so we don't want to hear different points of view. If you see the world this way, you'll have a strong incentive to bully people into not raising objections, but you'll also be hiding from the complexity of the real world.

Q: What are the major ingredients for a successful negotiation?

Patton: At a minimum, it's when your interests and the other side's interests are both met better than they would be with no agreement. Beyond that, an ideal agreement feels fair, legitimate, and justifiable, and it's easy to implement. Everything else being equal, a successful negotiation also improves your relationship with the other parties.

Q: What are some of the major pitfalls you see people fall into when they're negotiating?

Patton: The biggest one is that people haggle for their demands instead of understanding the interests underlying those demands and looking for creative ways to meet them. In any negotiation, the parties typically have some interests that are shared, some that are different and some that conflict. The goal is to maximize shared interests and to find creative ways, if possible, to meet the differing interests so both parties can get their interests met. And where interests are in conflict, the goal is to achieve a solution that both parties can accept, which is easiest if you focus on legitimate standards and setting a good precedent versus simple haggling.

Q: Can you give an example for how to negotiate for interests rather than demands?

Patton: Leading up to his election, Deval Patrick, the governor of Massachusetts, faced criticism for his position that children of illegal immigrants should qualify for in-state college tuition. His response was a model of what you want to do when responding to any hot-button issue. He basically said, look, this is a tough issue. On the one hand, we've got a very limited resource that ought to go to people who are here legally. We shouldn't be rewarding lawlessness or undercut the law. But at the same time, the children who came to Massachusetts unlawfully didn't have any choice in the matter and worked hard to obtain good grades to get into college. We want to compete as a state by developing a high-tech economy, and we're all going to be better off if these kids are educated and can contribute to our economy than if we tell them, I'm sorry, take it to the streets. Governor Patrick's response was successful because he acknowledged there are two sides to the issue, and he framed a response in terms of the interest of his audience of Massachusetts residents—lower crime and a stronger economy.

Q: You say in *Getting to Yes* that it's important to be tough on the problem but soft on the people. Why is that important, and how do you go about doing that?

Patton: You get in trouble when you implicitly say, "You're an idiot and I have the right answer." That's fundamentally disrespectful, and it builds resentment, which will only make your life harder. It's important to disagree without being disrespectful, and that means holding open the possibility that there's something you don't know. It's far more productive to say—provided you believe it, "Here's how I see it, and here's why I see it that way, but maybe there's something I'm missing." That's a far different approach from saying, "No, you idiot, that's wrong." You don't have to fake a lack of confidence. You can be 99 percent certain, just not 100 percent.

Q: When you negotiate, how can you identify the other party's interests?

Patton: You generally start by saying, "Why is that important to you?" Or you can ask, "What would be wrong with something like this?" That will implicitly get you information about interests. You can also pose a potential solution. "If we did something like this, would that be of interest?" Or you can give people a choice. "We can pursue this option or these other options." Which of these would be worth exploring from your point of view? When you negotiate, people aren't going to provide you a list of their interests. You need to put things in a context where people see a reason to talk to you about them.

Q: What one piece of advice do you have for PR people as they work to build consensus for their program?

Patton: Don't assume your point of view is necessarily right. I know that sounds incredibly counterintuitive. But if you see yourself as right, you're likely to push people to see that you're right, and then you're going to get pushed back and distract them from the merits of what you're saying. It's like teenagers. You get a lot of push back when you try to push them. It's much better to attract people to you by framing the problem in a way that matters to them and then seeking their feedback. Help them understand how you got to where you are. And then either implicitly or explicitly ask whether they see things differently, and if so, why and how. That is the most persuasive way I know to negotiate.

ADVANCING YOUR BUSINESS OBJECTIVES

Conversely, building consensus ensures that you stay on message once it's time to develop and roll out your PR plan. You can present your organization in a solidly unified way that advances the company's overall business objectives.

Take Skytap, an early-stage technology start-up founded by a group of computer scientists at the University of Washington. The company was developing its technology under the radar and was not yet ready to announce it. Nevertheless, executives wanted to build excitement for the company by announcing the fact that two leading venture capitalists in the Seattle area had invested in the company. In addition, executives wanted to leverage PR to attract high-quality job candidates to the company.

To ensure that everyone agreed on these objectives, Skytap Chief Products and Marketing Officer Steve Brodie met with the board of directors to achieve their buy-in. Ultimately, the board agreed and gave the green light to move forward with the program. Brodie then developed a plan and brought it back to board members for their review. "We wanted to make the board members available to the press to answer questions, so briefing them on what to expect and ensuring they were in alignment was important," he says.

By building consensus before rolling out the plan, Brodie ensured that everyone delivered the same messages without revealing too much or too little about the technology Skytap was not yet ready to announce. "It could have caused problems if one of the board members divulged more than we were prepared to, or if I divulged more," Brodie says. "And it could have been awkward if we gave different information to different publications and didn't give everyone a fair shake. Having everyone on board as to what we were and weren't going to say ensured that we stayed on message."

In the end, the approach worked beautifully. Skytap received coverage in nine publications, including the three it had targeted. In addition, several high-quality job candidates contacted Skytap as a result of the coverage, saving the company thousands of dollars in recruiting costs. "Coming to consensus as to what we were trying to achieve had huge payoffs," says Brodie. "We got a lot of positive press. In addition, our recruit flow has really gone up and the caliber has been much higher than what we were seeing in the past."

WHY COMPANIES SKIP THIS STEP

Our experience is that, despite the importance of building consensus, many executives tend to skip over this principle altogether. One reason is that they underestimate the value of PR. They may think the CEO and the board of directors don't care about PR. But that reasoning is shortsighted. When an article about your competitor appears in the *Wall Street Journal* and you're not included, the reality is that the CEO and board of directors are going to care. If you haven't obtained buy-in for PR in advance, all of a sudden you're going to have to do a lot of backtracking and may find yourself in a situation that undermines your success.

Another reason people fail to share their approach to PR is fear. They may fear that soliciting other people's opinions means they give up control over a strategy they feel strongly about, the concept that too many cooks spoil the broth. Or they may be afraid that if they talk about their program in advance, they'll be held accountable if it falls short of its intended goals.

This latter fear held back one of our former clients, a PR manager at a technology company. He didn't want to talk about his program and say, "I'm going to get these results." His fear was that he had no control over what articles editors were actually going to write, so he didn't want to be held accountable for the results.

While this fear may seem understandable on the surface, it will set you up for disaster in the long run. By failing to discuss the results you expect, you leave it up to people's imaginations who, in a vacuum, will set their own expectations for what coverage the company should be getting. While it may be your goal to garner coverage in ten highly targeted publications, at the end of the PR campaign the CEO may barge into your office and demand, "Why aren't we getting more coverage? My expectation was that we were going to have twenty-five articles!" To avoid the risk that you and others in your company are out of alignment, it's far smarter to discuss the PR program in advance, set expectations, and then reset them as factors change.

TIPS FOR OBTAINING BUY-IN

So how do you develop consensus for your PR program? The answer depends on the size of your organization and your specific role within it or at the agency for which you work. In all cases, however, the following seven tips apply:

1. *Identify all key stakeholders.* The first step is to identify the key stakeholders in the organization. This often comes down to who controls the strategic direction of the company and who controls the money. If the strategic direction of the company changes, your program must also change to mirror the company's new objectives. Therefore, it's critical to obtain buy-in from these key influencers. The CFO and the financial team may also control or influence the size of your budget. Therefore, they too need to understand the program and how it will advance the business objectives of the company.

    Institutional investors may wreak havoc on your program if they don't understand your approach. Therefore, it's also critical that the investor relations team be informed of the program. If you work with an outside PR agency, make sure your PR team is involved from the outset. Don't just develop the program and ask them to implement it. Capitalize on their expertise and involve them throughout the process. Finally, you'll want to discuss your program with employees. Whether you actually want to solicit their opinions is a company-by-company decision. At the very least, however, you'll want to educate employees so they understand the strategy and the reasons you've decided to pursue the specific objectives included in the program.

    The following is a checklist of the key stakeholders you should consider reaching out to as you build consensus for your program:

    *   Your direct manager
    *   The vice president of marketing

- The CEO
- The executive management team
- The CFO
- The board of directors
- The investor relations team
- Your outside PR agency or internal PR team
- The sales team
- Employees at all levels

2. *Obtain advance agreement about the budget.* Before developing a detailed PR plan, it's important to gain consensus as to what resources will be allocated to PR, both in terms of dollars and headcount. The amount may be a percentage of the total marketing budget, or it may be an arbitrary number. Whatever the total budget you end up with, it's important to put a stake in the ground by sharing some of your thoughts regarding the PR activities you may implement and what these are likely to cost.

   Developing a PR plan without knowing how much you have to spend is a waste of time. It's like an architect designing a house without knowing his client's budget. Is it going to be a $200,000 house or a $2 million house? The difference dictates the size of the house and the materials the builder can work with. In the same way, gaining agreement as to the size of the PR budget in advance helps you develop a more realistic PR plan that's in line with your company's resources.

3. *Understand their interests.* Understanding the interests of each stakeholder will enable you to successfully sell your PR program and develop a much stronger strategy in the long run. Before you approach any of the stakeholders in your company, it's important that you develop a deep understanding of their perspective so you focus on the aspects that matter to them most. Remember Nick Marshall, the advertising executive in the movie *What Women Want?* After an accident in the bathroom, he was suddenly able to hear women's thoughts. Getting into women's heads to understand what they want ultimately enabled him to win the Nike account. In the same way, a successful PR manager or executive will look for opportunities to get into the heads of key stakeholders to really understand their perspectives, objectives, and biases.

   For example, if you're discussing your PR program with the board of directors, you need to have a sense of what they want to see. Is their goal to see stock prices rise? Is it to see revenue grow by 10 percent over the next year? If you're talking to the CFO, is her goal to understand how much you're spending and what the return on investment will be? If you're addressing the sales team, is the team's goal to introduce the company product to a new market? It's critical that you develop an intimate understanding of each stakeholder's interests before you develop and implement your PR plan.

4. *Frame your pitch for each specific audience.* Once you understand the specific interests of each stakeholder, you need to tailor a pitch that addresses the specific issues each stakeholder cares about and show that your PR program will help accomplish those objectives. If the board of directors cares about revenue growth, talk about how PR will help increase revenue. If the CFO cares about ROI, talk about the cost of rolling out your PR campaign and the results you expect. If the sales team cares about attracting new customers, discuss how PR will bring that about.

   As you frame your pitch, remember that it is important to focus on interests, not position. As the authors point out in *Getting to Yes*, "When negotiators bargain over positions, they lock themselves into those positions. The more you clarify your position and defend it against attack, the more committed you become to it. The more you try to convince the other side of the impossibility of changing your opening position, the more difficult it becomes to do so."[3] Rather than digging in and taking a fixed position about your PR program, you will be more successful if you listen openly to understand the interests of each stakeholder, map their specific interests back to the goals PR will achieve, and focus on opportunities for mutual gain.

5. *Take a team approach.* Obtaining buy-in for PR is a team effort that will likely involve several people in the organization. No matter what your role is, you should always advocate that the PR program be shared broadly. For example, if you're a PR manager or specialist in a company, you'll need to gain the support from the vice president of marketing and convince him to obtain buy-in from the CEO and executive team. If you're the CEO, you should ask your PR team to share the PR approach it's considering so you understand it yourself and build consensus with the board and investors.

   If you're an account executive at an outside agency, it's your responsibility to recommend that your client obtain buy-in for the program from key stakeholders. Provide your client with the tools and recaps needed to make her job easy and offer to be present at critical meetings. Of course, you ultimately can't control the actions of your client. But at the very least you need to ask the question, "Have you talked to others in the organization about the approach we're considering?" Every savvy PR person knows how to influence. In the same way you influence the media, you need to convince your client to obtain buy-in for PR.

6. *Be open to feedback.* As you go about explaining your approach to PR and the results you expect to generate, be open to revising your program with the feedback you obtain. Our work with our client Big Fish Games illustrates the benefits of this approach. After outlining a general approach to PR for Big Fish, we held informal one-on-one meetings with all the key stakeholders, including the CEO, CFO, COO, vice president of development, and vice president of marketing. We then incorporated their feedback and met with all of these stakeholders in the same room to make sure they had bought into the uberstrategy we were proposing.

During this meeting, it became clear that various stakeholders had different opinions. For example, some executives thought we should publicize the new deals Big Fish signed to get their games sold at specific retail outlets while others believed this would only encourage the company's competitors to pursue those same partnerships. Some thought we should focus on broadcast to increase brand awareness for Big Fish Games while others believed that print was the best medium.

Holding the meeting created a lively dialogue that ultimately led to agreement. Once everyone agreed on the overall approach, we developed a detailed PR plan and presented it to the overall team in e-mail. We then followed up with stakeholders individually to make sure the plan addressed the specific issues they had raised.

Building consensus in this way enabled us to develop closer relationships with key stakeholders in the company. It also helped us solidify the company's objectives to ensure that everyone agreed with the overall strategy we were proposing. Ultimately this enabled us to concentrate our efforts on developing and implementing a solid plan rather than defending ourselves against the objections that often occur when you haven't worked ahead of time to obtain buy-in.

7. *Update stakeholders at regular intervals.* It's important to note that building consensus isn't a one-time effort. To be effective, it must be a continual process. If you're asking stakeholders early on for their buy-in and support but not circling back to update them later, it may appear that soliciting their buy-in was a token gesture and that you didn't respect the opinions you got.

Update them once you've developed the plan and again as you're implementing it. Frequently PR professionals wait until all the coverage has emerged before they provide an update, but that's often too late. In the absence of news, stakeholders may conclude that nothing is happening. Even if there are not yet any coverage results, you need to update stakeholders at regular intervals on the work you're doing behind the scenes. Ask stakeholders, "Would it be helpful if I circled back with you on a biweekly or monthly basis?" And then make sure you update them according to the timelines you've agreed upon.

Along the same lines, it's important to reset expectations as factors change. There's no way to anticipate everything that can affect your program. A new competitor might enter your industry, a hot new trend may focus the media in a different direction, or marketing conditions may shift, affecting the success of your program. By setting expectations at the outset and then resetting them as factors change, you'll keep stakeholders in the loop while preventing disappointment or surprise. (Please see Principle 8 for ways to maintain an open information flow as you implement your PR plan.)

A strategic approach to PR requires that you work to achieve buy-in for PR before you set out to develop and implement a detailed plan. Not only does building consensus ensure that everyone in the company is heading down the same path; it also elevates the importance of PR within the organization, heightening awareness of the critical role it plays in achieving your company's most important business objectives. To be successful, you have to be visible. And the time you spend upfront selling your PR program will keep you from spinning your wheels farther down the road.

SELECT YOUR PR TEAM WISELY

One of the most daunting questions a company can face is whether to go with an in-house PR staff, an external PR agency, or a mix of the two. Before making the decision, it's important to understand the pros and cons of each approach. It's also critical to learn how to evaluate a prospective PR team and what terms to establish to get the relationship off to a great start.

IN-HOUSE STAFF OR OUTSIDE AGENCY?
Under what conditions should you take PR in-house versus contract the work to an outside agency? The answer depends on the size of your budget, the needs of your company, and the degree of media interest in your organization.

"It's really a balance between your financial situation and how much work needs to be done," says Glenda Dorchak, CEO of Intrinsyc Software. "Companies that are narrowly focused on a specific technology may be able to handle the whole thing internally, whereas large companies trying to reach a wider range of audiences may want to contract out some of this work."

Pros of an In-House Approach
One of the biggest advantages of having an in-house PR professional is that it can be more cost-effective. It's very likely your company could hire a talented PR person for far less than the cost of paying an outside PR agency. And if you work for a small company with a limited marketing budget, you could

save even further by having your PR person wear multiple hats, perhaps handle marketing responsibilities in addition to PR.

Another advantage of hiring full-time PR professionals is the close working relationships they're able to forge with employees in your organization. Say you work for a high-profile company that receives a large volume of requests from the media. Because of the close relationships they've developed, in-house PR professionals know which experts to approach for each particular information request, making it easy for them to quickly respond to reporters' questions. Or say your organization is a hospital, university, or government institution that often draws reporters to your site. Having an internal PR staff makes it easy to accommodate requests for on-site visits while enforcing the policies your organization has in place.

Those on the internal PR team at Seattle Children's Hospital enjoy close relationships with hospital faculty and the local media, making it easy for them to serve the interests of both groups. Seattle Children's Hospital works with an external PR firm to build its national brand, but having a PR staff on-site also enables the hospital to provide the media with the information it needs during hospital visits while enforcing privacy and safety policies. "It's really helpful to have an internal PR staff that all the faculty know and feel comfortable with," says David Perry, vice president of marketing and communication at Seattle Children's Hospital. "Having a staff that people see on a daily basis assures everyone they're in good hands."

Alaska Airlines also relies mainly on an internal PR staff, turning to external counsel only in situations in which executives believe that an outside perspective would be valuable. "The idea is to have a core set of communicators who really know our company and who can establish long-term relationships with both internal and external stakeholders," says Caroline Boren, Alaska Airlines' managing director for corporate and strategic communications. "Hiring employees internally also allows us to develop a staff that can really communicate how Alaska Airlines works. They walk down the halls, they visit different places, and that enables them to gain a deep understanding of how we operate."

Advantages of an Outside PR Agency
While hiring an internal PR person is critical in some cases, one of the major advantages of working with an outside PR agency is the bank of knowledge it allows you to tap into. With a PR agency, you don't just get an individual, you get an entire team. The team of people assembled to handle your PR efforts collectively brings years of experience working on multiple accounts. In addition, it typically has tens or even hundreds of colleagues at the agency it can go to for advice when a difficult issue arises. Among the benefits of a team approach are the ability to brainstorm creative ideas, collectively address problems, and review each other's materials, all of which help to ensure that your company utilizes PR as effectively as possible.

Another advantage of hiring a PR agency is the fact that account executives work on multiple accounts and are constantly learning from the campaigns they're implementing on behalf of other clients. Because they frequently work on complementary accounts, they often learn of specific editorial opportunities relevant to your company that they otherwise wouldn't know about.

"An experienced PR agency has contacts in your particular industry with reporters whose job it is to write about your kind of product," says Rick Romatowski, former chief operating officer at Open Interface North America, a pioneer in Bluetooth technology. "By hiring these people out of house, you're leveraging their relationships, which can be tremendously beneficial."

A third reason to go with an outside PR firm is if your level of PR activity varies substantially over the course of the year. Perhaps you're launching a new product one month but have very little activity planned the following two. It might make more sense to work with an outside PR agency that can handle this variability rather than hiring a full-time PR manager and having a regular cost associated with that person. Or perhaps you work for a small company that doesn't have the time to manage an internal person daily. While managing an outside PR firm also requires time and energy, it is generally less time-consuming than overseeing an internal employee.

Big Fish Games contracts PR to an outside agency, something it has done since the casual gaming company was formed. "Our company has a fundamental belief that if it's not a core competency related to what we do, then it's better to partner with a best-of-breed company," says Paul Thelen, Big Fish Games founder and chief strategy officer. "We could try to build PR up as a core competency, but would we ever be the best PR company in the world? No. That's why we try to partner with a good company that already has the expertise and contacts."

THE HYBRID APPROACH

While both the in-house and out-of-house approaches have their advantages, we believe that, if your organization can afford it, a hybrid approach, in which a company has an internal PR staff that works together with an outside agency, is the best solution. Establishing a partnership between an internal PR team and an external agency helps to push PR efforts forward more seamlessly. Having an internal staff that really understands PR enables organizations to manage their external PR agency more effectively. With the PR wheels turning internally and externally, companies can accomplish their business objectives more quickly and nimbly than with either of the other two approaches.

In reality, however, most small and medium-size companies do not have the budget for both an internal PR staff and an outside agency. In many cases, organizations appoint a marketing manager to oversee their external PR agency.

This, too, can work well. However, if you work for a high-profile Fortune 100 company such as Microsoft or Starbucks that has a complex mix of PR needs, it's critical that you take a hybrid approach. Having an internal PR staff provides an efficient way to develop strategy and messaging while quickly responding to a high volume of information requests. Employing an outside PR agency adds focus where you need it, whether in specific geographical markets, market segments, or PR specialty areas such as public affairs or crisis communications. An external PR agency can also manage proactive PR campaigns while adding a greater range of expertise as you develop and refine your PR strategy.

If you do take a hybrid approach, it's crucial that you clearly divide the responsibilities to ensure that both your internal and external PR teams focus their efforts to achieve maximum impact. It's also important that you invite both teams to contribute to your overall PR strategy. Completely handing over strategy development to only one team will ruin the morale of the other while preventing you from capitalizing on the full range of expertise available to you. Allowing both your internal team and your PR agency to contribute to the overall strategy guarantees the strongest partnership while helping to ensure that you consistently take the best course of action.

Among the companies that take a hybrid approach to PR is Starbucks. In addition to employing an internal PR staff, Starbucks works with a national PR agency as well as a cadre of local PR firms with expertise in various geographical markets. This combination enables Starbucks to respond flexibly to information requests while giving the company the expertise it needs to proactively launch focused campaigns. "I think the combination is really effective," says Brad Stevens, former vice president of U.S. marketing at Starbucks. "Our internal staff has an inherent understanding of our brand, how we get things done, and who needs to be involved in decisions, which contributes a level of expertise that I think is hard for an outside agency to gain. On the flip side, our external agencies bring the outside perspective that helps us avoid tunnel vision. They help us see different perspectives and better understand how the public or media might react to something we're doing. The combination works really well."

Linden Lab, maker of the 3D digital online world Second Life, initially handled all of its PR in-house. But as the company became deluged with media requests about its Internet-based universe, executives decided to hire a global PR firm to help it with its efforts. In addition to establishing a PR team in the United States, the PR agency has set up teams in France, Germany, United Kingdom, and Japan. "There's no way we could do that internally," says Catherine Smith, senior marketing manager for Linden Lab. "We're coming up against cultural, legal, and technology issues that nobody's dealt with before, and I really needed somebody who could help me create a process for dealing with information requests, crisis communications, and all the different pieces that were sure to come."

Public Relations Agency Evaluation Scorecard

This is excerpted from the Council of Public Relations Firms' Hiring a Public Relations Firm: A Guide for Clients.

	A CUT ABOVE: 3 POINTS	THE RIGHT STUFF: 2 POINTS	JUST OK: 1 POINT	WEAK: 0 POINTS
CLIENT SERVICE				
Responsive during the review process				
Enthusiastic about what they do				
Committed to excellence in client service				
Measurement protocols				
Client references				
Approach to financial account management				
Understand industry				
Able to meet all our needs				
Subtotal				
DEMONSTRATED PERFORMANCE				
Case studies				
Creativity				
Strategic thinking				
Innovation				
Multi-stakeholder approach				
Accountability for results				
Subtotal				
ACCOUNT STAFF				
Qualifications				
Professional development				
Management skills				
Experience in our industry				
Personalities compatible with ours				
Subtotal				
AGENCY CHARACTER				
Mission and values of firm				
Serve multiple account needs seamlessly				
Established and proven				
Client conflicts discussed and resolved				
Industry recognition, awards				
Subtotal				
TOTALS				
Client Service				
Demonstrated Performance				
Account Staff				
Agency Character				

Other resources for hiring a PR firm can be found on the Council of Public Relations Firms Web site at www.prfirms.org.

WHAT TO EVALUATE

Once you've decided how to structure your PR efforts, the next step is to evaluate prospective PR teams to ensure that you hire the right people to move your business forward.

Share Your Business Objectives and Your Budget

Whether you're hiring an in-house PR staff or an external agency, you should be prepared to share your business objectives and your budget. When evaluating PR professionals, the most important thing to assess is whether they understand your business objectives and can develop creative ideas to help you achieve your goals. Share your objectives and problems, but don't tell them how to address the situation. Let them come up with the best strategies for you to evaluate. It's just like going to the doctor when you're sick. You don't tell your doctor how to treat you. You share your symptoms and let your doctor determine the best remedy. It's important that you choose a PR team in which you can establish that same trust.

A great way to determine whether the PR professional or firm you're considering understands your company's business objectives is to provide the individual or company with a specific business problem and test them on their thinking. As part of their request for proposals (RFP), many companies ask the PR firms they're evaluating to develop a specific approach in response to a business problem they're facing. Here are some business problems companies have asked PR firms to address during the RFP process:

- Develop a recommendation to help a company position itself as the organization of choice regionally and nationally.
- Create a PR program to help promote a new product.
- Share ideas to help a company establish itself as a thought leader in its category.

Once you give your candidates a real business problem, it becomes easier to compare and evaluate them more objectively. How thoroughly did they examine your company's business problem? How creative are the solutions they're proposing? Are their recommendations realistic based on your PR budget? The quality of solutions that prospective candidates develop during the interview process will demonstrate what they're truly capable of once on the job.

At the same time, Kathy Cripps, president of the Council of Public Relations Firms, counsels, "Be respectful of an agency's time. An effective relationship with a PR firm begins during your search."

She also encourages clients to consider the size of their PR expense budget. "A company with a $120,000 per year budget is going to have a different agency selection process than a company spending $500,000 to $1 million per year," she says. "Similarly, an agency competing for a multimillion dollar account is going to be willing to invest more to win a company's business. The bottom line is that any assignment given during a search should be proportionate to the budget, and the process needs to be fair and respectful for all the parties involved."

The Importance of Good Chemistry

Another factor to consider is chemistry. If you're evaluating a handful of reputable PR professionals or agencies, they may all come up with creative ideas to address your business problem. In the end, the biggest differentiator may be personal chemistry. Who's going to work best with the executives in your company? Who's going to fit into your company culture? Do you personally enjoy working with them? With many vendors, it's possible to work together effectively without ever developing a solid rapport. But because of the deep relationships a PR person must establish with executives at your firm, a solid rapport is highly important to the success of their efforts.

Personal chemistry was a key factor Knowledge Anywhere considered when selecting a PR firm. "You really have to be able to click with the people you work with in PR," says Bill Strelke, the company's former executive vice president of marketing and business development. "You have to trust them, they have to trust you, and quite frankly, you need to like each other. If they really understand your business and you personally, your PR firm will feel more comfortable suggesting creative ideas and telling you when they agree or disagree with the ideas you present. In the end, there's much more excitement about your mutual success."

Andrea Mocherman, marketing communications manager for SNAPin Software, agrees. "You just have to feel comfortable and confident with all the individuals working on your PR account team. To do its job well, your PR firm needs to understand the strengths and weaknesses of each of the executives as well as the internal workings of the company. In my opinion, it's just a different level of knowing somebody than any other type of vendor relationship."

Other Factors to Consider

In addition to evaluating PR practitioners based on chemistry and their understanding of your business, your company should consider a host of other factors in choosing a PR professional or PR firm:

- Is your business complementary with their current portfolio or clients?
- What experience does the PR person or firm have in your industry?
- Are they passionate about what you're doing?

- Are they asking smart questions throughout the process?
- Do they have the capability and bandwidth to do a good job?

If you're hiring a PR firm, you'll also want to consider whether it works with similar-size clients. It's great to be the largest client in the firm's mix because the firm will likely be attentive and devote senior people to your account to make sure they keep it. On the other hand, being a small fish in a big pond can be problematic. The firm may assign junior people to your account and keep shifting who is assigned to work with you. When a large client needs the firm's immediate attention, you might suddenly take a low priority.

When searching for a PR firm, Paul Thelen, founder of Big Fish Games, says his company originally chose a brand-name PR agency. Eventually, however, he decided the firm wasn't aggressive enough and switched to a smaller agency that worked more tenaciously to place stories in the media. "We wanted a PR firm that really understood what we're trying to accomplish with PR, and we wanted a team that was very proactive and aggressive about pushing to get contacts made and articles written."

Steve Brodie, chief products and marketing officer for Skytap, a technology start-up in Seattle, says his company wanted an agency that had worked with other start-ups, had experience in PR for enterprise-based Web products, and was flexible enough to work with a small but growing budget. "Also, I think a lot of it is just a personality issue and feeling like this is someone we could work with together effectively. They might have a long track record of success, but their style had to mesh with our style."

The Council of Public Relations Firms posts a public relations agency scorecard that many companies use when evaluating prospective firms. Although the scorecard was developed to assess external PR agencies, many of its factors are applicable to hiring an internal PR professional. Take the scorecard, tailor it to the specific needs of your company, and have it ready to go as you begin the evaluation process.

HIRING AN EXTERNAL PR AGENCY

Hiring an external PR agency is typically a two-step process that involves issuing and obtaining responses to your RFP and then inviting two or three PR firms to present their plans in person. To reach the best decision, you'll want to assemble a team of three or four people in the company who can help you evaluate prospective agencies. Depending on the type of PR program you're planning to implement, this should include the PR or marketing manager who will oversee the work of the agency, the vice president of marketing, and a couple of internal clients such as the chief financial officer, the human resources director, or a key brand manager. You'll also want to engage the CEO once you've narrowed down your list and have scheduled the presentations.

The Request for Proposal

The first step in selecting a PR agency is to develop a list of six to eight PR agencies you'd like to work with. You may want to ask around to learn what PR agencies other companies are working with and what their experiences have been. In addition, the Council of Public Relations Firms offers a "find-a-firm" section on its Web site that helps organizations identify PR firms based on their geographical location, size, and areas of expertise (www.prfirms. org/findafirm).

Once you've created a list of potential firms, you'll need to develop an RFP to send to each of the PR agencies on your list. Your RFP should include background about your organization, its mission and vision, a statement of the business problem you're asking the PR agency to address, and your deadline for receiving responses. It should also ask each agency to provide the following information:

- The PR agency's detailed description for addressing your business problem as well as the projected budget, results, and ROI
- Examples of relevant media placements and a description of the agency pitches used to obtain that coverage
- Team member bios, billing rates, and the percentage of time each team member will spend on your account
- A list of current clients as well as a list, with explanation, of clients lost in the past year
- A statement disclosing any potential conflicts of interest

Your internal team should evaluate each of these written responses with the goal of reducing your list to two or three PR agencies you'd like to have present in person. As the RFP process gets under way, be prepared to tell the PR agencies the names of other firms they're competing against. In addition, ask them to sign an agreement to keep all information discussed during the process confidential.

The In-Person Interview

Once you've developed a short list of two or three PR agencies, the second step is to invite them to present their plans in person. During these meetings, you'll want to pay particular attention to how each PR agency interacts with others on their team as well as with the people in your organization. Weigh the level of chemistry and the creativity in the responses to your questions. Also look for the teams' adaptability and ability to think on their feet, as well as their level of understanding and passion about your business. Ask the participants on your internal team to fill out a scorecard so they can compare each agency in an objective way.

After all the presentations are completed, your team should meet to evaluate each agency and select the one that best meets your needs. Before reaching a final decision, check the references of your first-choice agency for clients they are working with now and those they have lost in the last year. Call your agency of choice to let it know it won the contract. Then immediately contact the losing firms to thank them for their participation. During these calls, you should be prepared to give each firm an honest critique of their strengths and weaknesses so they can learn from the time they've invested in the process.

SELECTING AN IN-HOUSE PR TEAM

If you're hiring a PR person in-house, whom you should select depends on whether you plan to handle all of your PR internally or take a hybrid approach. If you're planning to do PR in-house, you'll need a PR person who excels at pitching stories to the media and can also handle PR both proactively and reactively. If you work for a small company, most likely you'll need someone who can juggle PR with other marketing functions and has skills that are complementary to the organization's marketing director. We recommend searching for a PR professional with five to seven years of experience working at a PR agency. Someone who has worked at an agency for that length of time should have substantial experience pitching stories to the media, developing and implementing PR plans, preparing executives for media interviews, and the other aspects of PR your company is likely to need ongoing help with.

If the PR person you hire will manage an external PR agency, you'll want to find a seasoned PR professional with experience managing a PR agency. Ask your job candidates if you can talk to a PR firm they've managed in the past. In addition, request samples of stories they've placed and ask them to walk you through the process they used for pitching these stories to each media outlet. Regardless of the person you're searching for, it's important to develop a set of key fundamental requirements and stick to them. In addition, make sure you have several candidates to choose from so that you can compare credentials, styles, approaches, and other factors.

GETTING THE RELATIONSHIP OFF TO A GREAT START

Congratulations, you've hired a winning PR team! Now that you've got your team on board, here are some of the processes you'll want to put into place to get the relationship off to a great start.

Defining the Terms of Payment

If you've hired an external PR agency, you'll need to agree on the terms of payment. While some companies prefer to pay their PR agency a set monthly retainer, we believe it's more equitable and better for both parties to set up a defined monthly scope of work but then pay for the actual time and materials your firm spends on your account. With a retainer, the hours spent working on your account inevitably turn out to be either more or less than the retainer you've agreed upon. As a result, either the company or the agency ends up with the short end of the stick. The better approach is to pay the agency for the hours actually worked with an agreement not to go over a maximum level without prior agreement. Most PR agencies should be adept at specifying the number of hours it takes them to perform work on a specific project and can provide an accurate cost estimate based on this assessment. If a project takes longer than expected, they can always circle back and explain why more hours are needed or scale back their plan to meet your budget constraints. We feel this approach builds in the greatest level of accountability.

The Kickoff Meeting

In addition to defining the terms of payment, you should hold a kickoff meeting with your internal PR team or external PR agency to decide on your priorities for the first 90 to 120 days. Invite key functional managers to discuss the business issues your company faces. Discuss your organization's business objectives and its PR efforts to date, including what worked and what failed. Educate the individual or PR agency about the nuances of the company as well as the personalities and opinions of key individuals. Ask them what they need from you to be successful. Clarify roles and responsibilities, and come to an agreement as to how you're going to measure success.

Establishing Regular Check-ins

After the kickoff meeting, your PR team should develop a detailed recap that calls out action items and next steps. You should also set up regular check-in meetings to receive updates, provide feedback, and discuss strategic issues affecting the company. Our experience is that twice a month works well for most companies, with more informal communication on a daily basis or whenever it's needed.

Granting Time and Access

To get the partnership off to a great start, it's also important that you give your PR team direct access to executives within your company. To do a good job, your PR team needs to be in the loop about what's happening inside your organization. That means sharing all important information with your PR team and inviting the team to participate in key strategy discussions that take place inside your company. It also means granting your PR team the freedom to e-mail executives within the organization as the need for information arises.

In addition, you should allow your PR team the time required to develop strategic plans. It's easy for company executives or the board of directors to get excited about an idea and want it implemented right away. While immediate action is sometimes necessary, obtaining the best results usually requires deliberate thought and planning. Allowing your PR team to work proactively to establish the right time frame for your PR efforts will help you to achieve the best results.

Although selecting a winning PR team requires a lot of work upfront, the biggest hurdle is figuring out what approach will work best for your organization. With a great PR team on board, you can now get to work utilizing PR to achieve your most important business goals. This starts with defining the exact audiences you seek to reach so that you can captivate them with maximum impact.

PRINCIPLE 3

KNOW YOUR TARGET AUDIENCES AND HOW TO REACH THEM

I t's a mantra we've all heard over and over again: know thy customer. While most companies understand who their target customers are, the difficulty lies in knowing how to reach them and doing so in a way that attracts attention. With PR, reaching your customers means working with the media outlets and analysts who reach your target audience. To accomplish this, you need to know both the right venue and the right person to contact at that venue.

Too often companies spend time creating and refining their messages only to deliver them to the wrong people. Nearly every journalist has experienced it, the daily barrage of e-mails from PR professionals who seem to have no idea what they write about. When PR practitioners make the same mistake too many times, they lose credibility. It's only a matter of time until every press release they send to a journalist winds up in the trash bin, unopened and unread.

If you have any doubt as to how many companies waste time pitching stories to the wrong audience, just ask Chris Anderson, editor in chief of *Wired* magazine. Anderson, who receives more than 300 e-mails from PR people a day, is so tired of wading through press releases from PR professionals who haven't taken the time to understand what *Wired* writes about that he took the dramatic step of blocking violators from contacting him and posting their e-mail addresses on his blog.

"I've had it," he wrote on his blog. "I get more than 300 e-mails a day and my problem isn't spam . . . it's PR people. Lazy flacks send press releases to the editor in chief of *Wired* because they can't be bothered to find out who on my staff, if anyone, might actually be interested in what they're pitching."[1]

This is a controversial move for sure. Yet it illustrates an important point: the failure to target one's message is not only completely ineffective, it also seriously damages a company's relationship with the media. So why do so many organizations make this mistake? In many cases, they haven't done enough planning. They only have only a vague understanding of where their customers go for information. What's more, they haven't done enough research to figure out what types of stories these media outlets cover or exactly whom they reach. In other cases, companies believe e-mailing press releases en masse will lead to the best results, meaning the largest volume of coverage. The reality is that such a vast quantity of coverage doesn't necessarily equal success. Nor does bombarding reporters with one press release after the next, leaving it up to them to determine which ones are newsworthy and relevant to the publication's audience.

"A strategic approach to PR isn't about quantity; it's about quality," says Keith Lindenburg, director, national public relations, Deloitte Services LP. "It's really a rifle approach versus a shotgun approach. You need to be very, very focused about who you want to reach and what messages you want to deliver to achieve your company's business objectives. If your goal is to win additional business in Columbus, Ohio, it may be far more helpful to place a bylined article in a local publication than it would be to secure a story on the national level."

DOING YOUR HOMEWORK

So how do you go about targeting your customers and doing so in a way that produces results? Simply put, you need to do your homework. First, you need to understand who your target audience is. For most companies, this isn't a problem. They usually have a deep understanding of their target audience that includes the age range of their customers, how much money they make, where they're located, and other vital demographic information. If you're a PR professional, make sure you understand exactly whom your clients want to reach and why. And if your clients don't know, encourage them to conduct some research to find this information.

Once you understand your target audience, you need to learn where these customers go for information and how best to position your news to make it interesting to each media outlet through which you plan to tell your story. Simply knowing what news sources your customers go to for information isn't enough. You need to research each target publication to understand what kinds of stories it covers and then find an angle that fits with each publication's specific interests.

For example, we recently pitched several stories about Mystery Case Files, a series of games developed by our client Big Fish Games. The goal was to broaden interest in Big Fish Games' casual games among Americans aged thirty-five years and older who are searching for entertainment yet don't consider themselves computer-savvy. Among our target publications were *Reader's Digest* and *USA Today*. Both of these magazines reach millions of people, yet each publication has a very different focus.

We conducted some initial research using Cision's media database and learned that *Reader's Digest* is dedicated to celebrating ordinary people doing extraordinary things. It also strives to deliver a compelling mix of humor with personal and other human interest stories. *USA Today* has 3.6 million readers, many of them affluent, well-educated professionals. Realizing this, we pitched completely different stories tailored to each publication. Our pitch to *Reader's Digest* focused on an ordinary woman named Judith Hunt who got her dog featured in Mystery Case Files by entering a contest hosted by Big Fish Games. The story we placed in *USA Today* promoted Mystery Case Files as a unique holiday gift idea. While both stories helped us achieve our goal of promoting Big Fish Games to a broader pool of potential customers, we applied two very different approaches to appeal to the two publications.

In addition to knowing your target audience and the media outlets that influence them, taking a strategic approach to PR requires staying current on the latest media trends. The Internet, satellite radio and television, TiVo, and other technologies are changing the way traditional media outlets operate. Reaching your audience requires a thorough understanding of the pressures facing traditional media outlets amid the sea changes taking place today.

This chapter discusses some of the trends—industry analysts, print publications, and broadcast media—that affect traditional media outlets, showing readers how to reach their customers using these options as the media world continues to transform itself. Principle 4 continues the discussion by exploring how to leverage search engine optimization, blogs, podcasts, videocasts, social networking sites, and other Web technologies to influence your customers in new and innovative ways.

THE INDUSTRY ANALYSTS

Regardless of the industry you're in, it's important to develop relationships with market research analysts and other industry experts who wield tremendous influence over the way your company is perceived in the marketplace. In the technology sector, hundreds of analyst firms have popped up over the years, spawning a multibillion-dollar industry. In other industries, market researchers, book authors, university professors, economists, sociologists, lawyers, and other experts can greatly influence how your company, product, or service is perceived.

Industry analysts influence customers in a variety of ways. They serve as consultants to customers deciding which products to purchase. They talk to customers informally about what's happening in the industry. They write and sell reports about industry trends. They're frequently quoted as experts in the media. And they often appear on panels at industry conferences, or they moderate panels in which they play a role in choosing the other panel participants.

To build credibility for your company, products, and business model, it's critical to maintain regular communication with key industry analysts. It's a good idea to initiate contact with industry analysts well in advance of your launch when your product, service, or even your company is in the development stage. Engaging analysts early in the process will enable you to obtain the critical input you need to shape your final offering. Expect to receive feedback regarding the overall category, the competition, and the issues your company must address to be successful. Analysts often ask some tough questions you may not have thought of. Taking these questions to heart will help you roll out a more compelling product or service to the media.

When you're ready to launch your product or service, you may be able to recommend some of these analysts to the media as a way to validate your client's perspective on the direction of your company or industry trends. Keeping analysts briefed about your company will increase your chances of being mentioned in the analyst reports many customers rely upon for their purchasing decisions. It may also make it possible to participate in a greater number of industry panels, helping to build broader awareness for your company.

It requires advance research to determine which industry analysts are most influential in your category. Sift through articles written about your industry during the last two years to learn which analysts are most frequently quoted. Research speaking opportunities in your industry to find out which analysts speak about topics relevant to your company. Obtain analyst reports to see which analysts write about your category and what they're saying.

Tips for Working with Analysts

The following is an interview with Iain Gillott, founder and president of iGR.

Q: How has the rise of the Internet changed the way analysts work?

Iain Gillott: What has changed is how analysts collect and deliver information. Back in the old days, you used to call up a company and ask them to send a press kit. So if you were researching five or six companies, it would take a while to get it all together because you'd have to call them up and then wait for the mail. We'd then write a research report, have it edited, proofread, printed, and bound and then mail it out. So the time between finishing a report and getting it in the hands of the client could be six weeks to two months. Now you can finish a report in a few days if you need to. So you can react much faster to what's happening in the industry.

Q: Has the Internet changed the way companies ought to work with analysts?

Gillott: It's very hard to hide these days. With e-mail, instant messaging, and cell phones, it's very easy for people like me to get ahold of executives at AT&T or Verizon, for example. If a company comes to me and says they've got all this business with AT&T or they're a strategic vendor, I can find out very quickly if that's true. And I can find out what people think of them very, very quickly. So as a company, you've got to be very careful about trying to build things up into what they're not. You'll get caught. And that's a big change I think from what it used to be like.

Q: What are the biggest frustrations you encounter when working with companies?

Gillott: The biggest frustration I have is when people brief us once a year. I probably get briefed by fifty to a hundred companies, so you can't expect me to remember what you were talking about a year ago. You need to build a relationship with the analyst, which means picking up the phone and updating me once a month about new developments. Another frustration is lack of relevancy. Just this morning, I got a press release from a company based in Los Angeles saying it opened up an office in San Francisco. I have no idea why that's newsworthy, so I instantly deleted it.

It's also frustrating when companies quote my competitors. I can't count the number of presentations I get where people say, "According to Gartner, the wireless market is expected to grow 300 percent, and company XYZ is perfectly positioned to take advantage of this growth." If you're trying to get business with Ford, would you walk in there and tell them how wonderful General Motors is? Well, you've just pitched me by quoting a competitor of mine, so why should I pay attention to you?

Q: What kinds of information do you want to hear from companies?

Gillott: In the initial meeting, I want to know background. What's their business model, and where do they get their funding? I want to know what they're doing, who their customers are—basically everything they can tell me about the company. With subsequent meetings, I just need an update. They need to say, "In our last briefing we told you we'd be announcing three new customers in the next quarter. Well, now we've got them. The customers are X, Y, and Z, and here's what we're doing for them." It's just a simple fifteen-minute conversation.

Q: What do you think of non-disclosure agreements (NDAs)?

Gillott: I prefer them actually because if you give me an NDA, you can tell me all the secret stuff, which makes the briefing so much more valuable. The last thing an analyst is going to do is break an NDA because if they do, they're out of business. At the same time, people say, "What use is an NDA to you since you can't use the information?" But you can use it. There's background information you can use, and it helps you see the major trends happening out there. NDAs are also helpful for companies because once you've made the announcement, you've got an independent spokesperson sitting there who knows the whole history of what was done and why it happened.

AT&T Wireless made a very smart move about a decade ago when it was developing the PocketNet phone, the first phone with a browser. The company invited about twelve analysts from different firms to sit on the Wireless Data Division Analyst Council. We met once a quarter and had big discussions about strategy. It was all very strictly controlled under NDA, but the level of access we had was phenomenal. Six to nine months later, when AT&T announced PocketNet, they gave the list of our names to the press and said, "Call them." We knew exactly what was happening and why, and AT&T knew exactly what we'd say. It was brilliant PR on their part.

Q: How should a company frame its product or service differently for an analyst than it would for a journalist?

Gillott: The briefing needs to include more depth and more technical background. When you think about a journalist who writes for a Web site, they're going to write something every day, and they've probably got about 200 words they can dedicate to any one story. Analyst reports are anywhere from 5,000 to 10,000 words, and we may take weeks to write them. I want to know all the background and technical detail, and I'm going to ask you.

Q: What feedback can companies expect to hear from you?

Gillott: A lot of times people will say, "We're going after the consumer market. We're going to get our software onto the handset by having consumers download it." And I'll say, "What about mobile operators? You've got to have friends among the mobile operators. Otherwise, they'll kill you." Or if they already have a strategy of working with the operators, I'll help them tweak it. I'll say, "If you're going after AT&T, you really want to stress this, but if you're going after Nokia, you'll want to take this approach instead." So my feedback can be both very strategic and very tactical.

Q: What advice do you have for PR professionals working with analysts?

Gillott: If you want a relationship with me, call me up. Don't send me e-mail. And don't have your eighteen-year-old summer intern call me. Give me someone experienced. Always include slides as part of the briefing. If you're trying to describe a software system to me, I need to be able to see it. And if you send it to me in advance, I'll run through it on my own, so when we're on the call, we can focus on the parts I'm most interested in. Also, don't try to be the technical guy or the sales guy. To me, a PR person should introduce the company, represent the company, but not be the company. That's the job of the company's executives. The PR person should make the introductions, take the notes, and make sure there's follow-up after the meeting.

Once you've identified the analysts most influential in your category, the goal is to help them understand your solution well enough so they can accurately describe it to others. Before going into the briefing, make sure you know what the analyst firm does to make money. Some analyst firms work only with vendors. Others write only research reports. Others focus on quantitative and qualitative research. Knowing the analyst firm's focus will help you position your story in the most compelling way.

Similarly, it's important to gather as much information as possible about each analyst's perceptions, opinions, and biases. Read the analyst's biography, the reports she has written, and her quotes in the press. Speak openly about your company's strategic road map and long-term goals, and always ask the analyst for her opinion. Finally, make sure you reinforce the relationship by keeping in touch after the briefing and providing updates about company developments as they unfold.

"The biggest frustration I have is when people brief us once a year," says analyst Iain Gillott, who owns his own firm, iGR. "I probably get briefed by fifty to one hundred companies, so you can't expect me to remember what you were talking about a year ago. You need to build a relationship with the analyst, which means picking up the phone and updating me once a month about new developments."

In addition to working with traditional industry analysts, there are times when you'll want to engage a book author, sociologist, university expert, or another influential to offer a third-party perspective on a story you're pitching. For example, when we pitched stories about Big Fish Games' Mystery Case

Files, we contacted an author of mystery novels in addition to industry analysts who follow the gaming industry. The goal was to brief the mystery novelist on the game and offer her as a resource to publications describing why women are drawn to mysteries. By briefing the mystery writer and gaining her agreement to speak to the media, we were able to obtain third-party validation to support the trend story we were pitching. This, in turn, made it a more compelling story for the reporters we were targeting.

TARGETING THE PRINT MEDIA

Reaching your customers through print publications can be a great way to build awareness for your company, product, or service, provided you understand the audience you're trying to reach and what it reads. National and city newspapers, city business journals, trade publications, association newsletters, and business and consumer magazines all reach specific audiences. As a PR professional, your work is very similar to that of an investigator. The goal is to identify the publications read by your audience and then arrive at an angle that will attract its interest.

Cision's media database can be a great resource for learning the exact circulation of each publication, what kinds of stories it covers, and information about the readership. Another way to find information about the publication is to request an advertising kit. These kits, created to help advertisers understand the publication's target audience, include editorial calendars as well as detailed information about the publication's readership. Finally, it's important to develop a solid understanding of each publication's major competitors. A consumer who reads *Better Homes and Gardens* probably doesn't also subscribe to *Sunset Magazine*. Knowing a publication's top competitors will enable you to reach all of your customers by developing a different story angle for each publication.

Working with Newspapers

As online publications become more prevalent and Internet advertising more sophisticated, traditional media publications are undergoing dramatic changes. Nowhere are these changes more profound than in the world of newspapers. During the past several years, newspaper advertising revenues have been declining precipitously thanks to the continuing shift of classified advertisers from print to online venues, especially to free sites such as Craigslist. To compensate, newspapers continue to cut costs by laying off employees, reducing benefits, and shrinking the physical size of their print publications. As ad revenues are declining, so too is readership. Since 1990, the number of U.S. daily newspapers has decreased from about 1,600 to 1,400, according to the

Newspaper Association of America.[2] During the same period, total newspaper circulation has been reduced from 62 million to 55 million.[3]

Many newspapers now compensate for these losses by investing more resources in their Web sites. This has enabled them to compete more effectively with cable television by posting breaking news instantaneously and then updating these stories throughout the day as more information emerges. As PR professionals work with online publications, it's important that they time the release of their stories closely.

The trend of newspapers moving more of their news online has implications for the way they receive feedback. Customers can now interact with editors, reporters, and other online users, posting their comments right beneath the story in bloglike style. In some cases, stories receive hundreds and even thousands of comments, prompting responses from the newspaper's reporters. This interactive feedback mechanism makes it more important than ever for a company's claims to be accurate and truthful. For example, if your company is cited in an article touting the quality of your customer service yet your customers aren't able to reach you, the truth is going to emerge quickly through customer comments. As a PR professional, you need to be able to stand behind the accuracy of every claim you make. You also need to follow the trail of customer comments to understand what customers are saying about your company, make sure their comments are accurate, and find creative ways to respond when they're not.

When newspapers lay off staff, the reporters who remain are increasingly rushed and overworked. They're writing fewer stories as the size of newspapers shrinks, focusing only on topics most relevant to their readers, which can make it harder for PR professionals to place stories. On the other hand, it can also work in your favor if you develop a solid pitch. For example, when pitching the Mystery Case Files story to the *Seattle Post-Intelligencer*, we made sure we provided all the components the reporter needed to write the story quickly. We offered her an angle, interviews with Big Fish Games executives, visual images of the game, and access to the game itself. To provide color and a balanced point of view, we also provided her with an interview with the mystery novelist, access to industry analysts, and statistics corroborating the trend story we were pitching. With reporters increasingly strapped for time, developing a solid pitch that includes all the components the reporter needs to write the article greatly increases your chances of placing a story.

Targeting Magazines and Trade Publications
With circulation often in the millions, business and consumer magazines can be a productive target for your story pitch. In addition, trade publications, with their well-defined niches, can be a useful vehicle for influencing your customers. Although they are not as hard hit by declining ad revenues as

newspapers, many print magazines and trade publications have added an online component while some publications have abandoned their print versions altogether.

In the technology sector, for example, *Computerworld* breaks news online first and then repackages a portion of this news for its print version. *InfoWorld* has taken a more radical approach, having discontinued its print component in 2006. Meanwhile, the Web-based technology media company TechTarget is moving into the print publication world. In 2004, it launched *CIO Decisions*, a new print magazine targeted at senior-level IT executives. And the IT professional organization British Computer Society continues to offer its magazine, *ITNOW* (formerly the *Computer Bulletin*) in print format after an extensive membership survey found that members still prefer to receive it that way.[4]

To work effectively with these publications, it's important to understand the details of how they operate and how they've integrated their online and print versions. Does the publication break news first in its print publication or the online version? Does it reprint news published in one medium in the other, or does each contain different content? Do both media share editorial staffs, or must you pitch stories to two editors at the same publication?

In addition to figuring out how magazines and trade publications integrate their print and online components, it's important to learn how they produce their content. While some specialized publications hire their own staff to write articles, others rely heavily on bylined articles from industry experts. Submitting bylined articles can raise awareness of your company while positioning your CEO as a thought leader in the category. Again, do your homework to understand the types of bylined articles your target publication is seeking. Request a copy of the writing guidelines as well as examples of other contributed articles the publication regards as successful.

Tips for Working with the Print Media

The following is an interview with Matt Slagle, PR manager with Sony Online Entertainment and former reporter for the Associated Press.

Q: What trends have you seen taking place in print journalism?

Matt Slagle: You're seeing declining newspaper subscriptions and a massive shift from newsprint to the online world. The biggest challenge is keeping those readers. As a result, you're seeing newspapers devoting more resources to online publications as readership goes down.

Q: How is the fact that readers can now provide immediate feedback to reporters' stories changing the way reporters work?

Slagle: It really opens up the dialogue between reporters and readers, which I think is great. Reporters and readers are linked together more closely than ever before.

Q: As a reporter, how many blogs did you monitor?

Slagle: I monitored dozens of blogs on a daily basis. They're becoming a very influential and powerful area of journalism. It's amazing the number of eyeballs that blogs are getting and the power they now wield with readers and companies. It's significant.

Q: Did you often use blogs as the basis of your stories?

Slagle: Sometimes they're the basis of your stories, sure. But more often they provide pieces of the story. There might be something mentioned in the blog that you hadn't considered and that might provide another element in the story you're already working on.

Q: An increasing number of reporters are starting their own blogs. Was that something AP reporters were asked to do?

Slagle: That's something we were increasingly asked to do, depending on the need. I think the blogging idea is an interesting one for reporters. When you write a traditional story, oftentimes you have a whole notebook full of information that didn't quite fit within your story. With a blog, you have the unique opportunity to touch upon all of these other issues and comment on them. Blogs also allow for a much more casual conversation than traditional stories with their formal structure, and that makes you more approachable.

Q: How are podcasts and videocasts changing the way reporters work?

Slagle: From a reporter's perspective, I think they've really broadened the expectations for a story. Traditionally you were limited to a text-only piece, a photographer took the pictures, and that was the end. Now you have all these new tools, which allow you to tell stories in new ways. It's really exciting.

Q: Should companies work with reporters differently as a result of these new media?

Slagle: It's more than just words now. The news itself may not be enough. You need to think visually and have some compelling visuals or sound to deliver along with your news.

Q: In what other ways has the Internet changed the way reporters work?

Slagle: At AP, the Internet has changed everything. We had to think about deadlines in a new way. Prior to the rise of online journalism, we were already a fast-paced company writing on minute-by-minute deadlines. With the Internet, we had to speed that process up even further because one second can make the difference between having the story first or having it third. The competitive pressure with the Internet is just incredible. At the same time, you can reach vast new audiences, and you can really tell stories in new ways. It's definitely been a sea change.

Q: How do these new deadline pressures change the way PR people ought to work with reporters?

Slagle: PR people should know that the deadlines are really tight and that the time constraints required to deliver news now are extremely high. They also need to be sensitive to the fact that reporters have even less time to respond immediately to phone calls or e-mail.

Q: As a reporter, what were some of the biggest frustrations you encountered working with PR people?

Slagle: I would say the biggest frustration was when PR people weren't aware of my beat or what I covered and pitched me stories that should have gone to someone else. Another frustration was getting the same pitch from two different people in the same company. Oftentimes, a company person and someone from the company's PR agency would call me with the exact same pitch. That would get frustrating. I was never opposed to a PR person calling me up to ask, "What are your interests? What are your beats?" First, it served as a good introduction to that person. Second, it helped to lay the groundwork for a good relationship in the future.

Q: How do the best PR people approach their jobs?

Slagle: The best PR people are the ones who knew me as a reporter and had a good sense of what I wanted and didn't want. They didn't call me and waste my time. It's a relationship. I needed to know I could trust the person to tell me stuff and that I could call them if I had a question or something urgent came up. So it goes both ways.

Q: Has your PR position with Sony changed your perspective about PR and the media?

Slagle: Absolutely. PR is a lot different from journalism. It involves a lot more planning. As a journalist, all you see is the end product of all the background work—a press release or a story pitch, for example. On the PR side, your job is to get everything ready for reporters and to make their job as easy as possible, and it's a lot of work. You're still pitching stories and building relationships, but the planning process is much different. It's been eye-opening for me.

REACHING YOUR AUDIENCE THROUGH BROADCAST

Often overlooked by companies, radio and television offer effective ways to reach thousands and even millions of customers. As with the print media, you need to make sure your story pitch matches the interests of the show on which you wish to appear. There's no better way to familiarize yourself with the format and content of a show than to sit down with a bowl of popcorn and watch or listen to several programs back-to-back. Susan Harrow, media coach and author of *The Ultimate Guide to Getting Booked on Oprah*, recommends recording two to four weeks of *Oprah*. "Then, sit down in a comfy spot and watch them all at once," she writes. "This will give you a sense of what's hot on *Oprah* for the next few months. (It does change and the key topics are featured in cycles.)"[5]

Another good source of information is the show's Web site. For example, Oprah's Web site, www.oprah.com, offers archived shows, book titles featured on the show, topics of upcoming programs, and her entire wish list of subjects. Similarly, if you're interested in *60 Minutes*, you can find important background information about the show by visiting www.cbsnews.com. The Web site offers information about the show's focus, correspondent bios, full-length *60 Minutes* podcasts, and sample videocasts, providing a good sense of the show's format and the types of stories it covers.

In addition to obtaining an in-depth understanding of the show's content, you'll need to think strategically about the show's viewers. What is their age range? What are their interests? By reading *PRWeek*, for example, you'll find that the average age of a *60 Minutes* viewer is fifty-three and that the show's youngest correspondent is sixty-one.[6] That in itself tells you a lot about how to go about pitching a story. You'll also learn that the size of the *60 Minutes* audience has been declining, another good piece of information to have for your pitch.

"If you're going to pitch anything, be a student of the broadcast to see what kinds of stories they're airing," says media, business, and executive coach Elaine Long. "You can learn a lot about the audience the newscast is targeting just through the story selection, so watch and listen."

Finally, you'll want to figure out which producers to contact with your story pitch and start to form relationships with them. This isn't as straightforward as with the print media, where beat reporters consistently cover the same topic. With television, you can sometimes find the producer for each segment of the program by watching the list of credits at the end of the show. Or you can call or e-mail the program's assignment desk and ask for the right person.

Working with the Broadcast Media

Perspectives from four broadcast experts

MARK LODATO, NEWS DIRECTOR AND PROFESSOR, CRONKITE SCHOOL OF JOURNALISM, ARIZONA STATE UNIVERSITY.

Q: What trends are you seeing in broadcast journalism?

Mark Lodato: First, the word broadcast is becoming less and less relevant. As technology evolves, consumers are able to custom-cast their news, information, and entertainment with podcasts, RSS feeds, and digital voice recorders. Citizen journalism continues to grow with "I reports" and "U reports" and of course online blogs. This ability to directly communicate back and forth with the audience creates new challenges for broadcast journalism, which must decide where to draw the line between what is legitimate journalism versus opinion or gut reaction. Some may argue that there is less good broadcast journalism out there. I disagree. I think there is just as much, if not more, quality visual journalism going on in America and elsewhere. It's just more fragmented.

Q: Are broadcast reporters covering the news differently than they once did?

Lodato: Of course, the basic tenants of good journalism remain the same, with reporters looking to produce accurate, well-written visual stories on deadline. But each day as more people come to rely on the Internet as their primary source of news, the broadcast reporter's job slowly shifts online as well. In the field, that means every reporter works for a twenty-four-hour news outlet. Instead of holding that key piece of information for a live report at 6 p.m., more reporters are getting in the habit of phoning that information into the Web producer right away and breaking news online.

MASON ESSIF, SENIOR VICE PRESIDENT AT OGILVY PUBLIC RELATIONS WORLDWIDE AND A FORMER BROADCAST PRODUCER/REPORTER FOR CNN, PBS, AND ABC NEWS.

Q: How has the Internet changed the broadcast landscape?

Mason Essif: As TV replaced newspapers as the source of breaking news, so too will the Internet replace TV as the source for breaking news. As newspapers responded to the usurpation by bringing more depth and news analysis to its audience, likewise TV will find itself bringing viewers a unique and more informed perspective, analysis, or angle.

Q: What kinds of pressures do broadcast journalists face in this new climate?

Essif: Since the proliferation of news outlets and the ability for anybody to be able to shoot, write, edit, and broadcast their own story, even if it's just on the Internet, reporters are under a tremendous amount of pressure to not only get the story right but to get the story first or to get the exclusive interview or the angle or perspective that nobody else has. You're always on a deadline.

Before CNN, broadcasters had time to gather the right elements, put their stories together, and air their stories at the end of the day. With the advent of CNN and cable TV, all that has changed. When I was at CNN in the early days, people would ask me, "What's your deadline?" and I would say, "As soon as you give it to me, I can put it on the air." This immediacy has become even more acute with the advent of the Internet and the ability to break a story to the world within seconds of shooting and typing.

DIANE DIMOND IS A VETERAN TV AND RADIO ANCHOR AND INVESTIGATIVE REPORTER WHO HAS WORKED AT BOTH THE LOCAL AND NATIONAL LEVEL, INCLUDING NBC, COURT TV, FOX NEWS, HARD COPY, WCBS-TV, AND NATIONAL PUBLIC RADIO. SHE IS AUTHOR OF *BE CAREFUL WHO YOU LOVE: INSIDE THE MICHAEL JACKSON CASE.*

Q: What are the major challenges television and radio stations face today?

Diane Dimond: In order—money, money, the Internet challenge, and money. The rising costs of new technology, shrinking advertising revenues, and the overall economic downturn have caused news divisions to lay off reporters all over the country. In the end, it's the viewers and listeners who suffer. They aren't being adequately served and are not getting the information they deserve from news organizations.

Also, there's the insidious problem of where to get future talent. These days there are few training grounds left for those aspiring to become reporters. The reality is stations are hiring inexperienced reporters for very little money and throwing them out into the streets with little real-life training. Mentors are few and far between because the experienced reporters are being fired because they've risen in the ranks and make too much money. We're left with newbie reporters who don't cover or uncover many complicated stories—just the accidents, fires, school board meetings. Again, the public loses.

Q: Given the changing broadcast landscape, do PR people need to work with you differently than they once did?

Dimond: I wince when I suggest this, but dumb it down for us. Reporters today are under such stress and deadline pressures—some cover two or three stories a day—that they need the information laid out for them in a nice, neat package. A tight one-page overview really helps. Any video, photographs, graphic art, charts, or audio bites—anything to help us look smart ensures we'll come back to you the next time. Think about producing a DVD full of these elements to hand out to each reporter.

Also, PR people need to really work with whoever the spokesperson is. Hire a media consultant for them if need be. You'd be amazed how many companies do this. Your goal is to get the spokesperson to be conversational, speaking in short sentences and equipped to handle any and all questions that might be asked. If you're working with a company that's had a problem, warn them ahead of time that there are going to be tough questions asked and if they gloss over them or stammer and stutter their way through the answer, that is what will make the news. I've sat at news conferences in the past where I thought, "Oh, man! This person who is speaking is awful—how will I ever make a story out of this?" Just because the CEO is available doesn't mean he or she is the right person to face the press.

KEVIN ESSEBAGGERS, ANCHOR AND REPORTER WITH WWTV/WWUP IN NORTHERN MICHIGAN.

Q: What are some of the pressures broadcast reporters face today?

Kevin Essebaggers: The time demands placed on reporters are increasing. Many stations are adding newscasts, and that means reporters need a fresh angle on their story several times a day. Reporters may also have to produce Web and print versions of stories if they work in a converged media environment.

Q: What are some of the biggest frustrations you encounter working with PR people?

Essebaggers: Some PR people seem to be available and overwilling to help when they have a positive story to pitch, but when their organization is involved in anything that can be perceived as even remotely negative, you can't reach them. It's a frustration that immediately reveals the character of a PR person and, therefore, the organization he or she represents. Another frustration for journalists can be a PR person who seems unnecessarily paranoid that the "media is out to get them." This type will try to require a list of questions before the interview, try to control the placement of your camera, or be otherwise difficult for no apparent reason.

Finally, there's the PR person who doesn't seem to understand the demands of the broadcast schedule. Planning a press conference for 4:45 p.m. when a reporter needs to have a story packaged for the 5 p.m. news does not work. Neither does planning a two-hour tour when a five-minute interview is all the reporter needs for their story. Deadlines are ultraimportant for broadcast journalists, and wasting our time is ultrafrustrating.

Q: What advice do you have for PR professionals trying to get their stories placed on TV and radio?

Essebaggers: When you want to get a story on TV, provide the reporter with a human element. Find a character for the story, and offer him or her to the reporter. Often your organization's story is best told through the people most involved or affected. Spokespeople are rarely the people most involved or affected. In fact, many stations strive to avoid "official sound" or "GITs: guys in ties." When pitching your story, tell me how your news will impact my viewers. This is where you put on the salesperson hat. If you can't figure out why the story is important or interesting for those outside your organization, then a reporter will not be likely to cover it.

Secondly, give me something visual. A board meeting does not make compelling television. The impact of a decision made at that board meeting may be very visually compelling. Look for opportunities that are not gimmicky, but add a visual component that best demonstrates the story.

Changes in the Broadcast Landscape

As with the print media, technology is radically altering the broadcast landscape. For one, TiVo and other devices known as digital video recorders (DVRs) are increasingly used by consumers to weed out television commercials. And as the leading national broadcast networks lose ad revenues, they are eagerly searching for new advertising models to compensate for these losses.

In addition, traditional radio and television programs face fierce competition from newer media such as satellite and cable broadcast, high-definition radio, and TV and Internet podcasts and videocasts, all of which are luring people away from the dial and the tube. A 2008 survey released by Deloitte found that one-third of all American consumers are watching TV shows online and that 45 percent of consumers are creating personal content for others to see.[7] As consumers embrace newer technologies, companies have been forced to navigate a more splintered landscape, reaching out to a larger number of media outlets to disseminate their news. The plus side of this development is that this fragmented landscape has made it possible for companies to focus their news on the exact audiences they seek to reach.

For example, the more than 200 satellite radio stations and 1,200 new high-definition radio channels that exist in the United States all attract a highly specialized niche audience, making it possible for companies to take a far more targeted approach with their stories. Rather than disseminating your message to a broad group of listeners or viewers, you can target the specific types of customer you seek to reach. This makes it easier to successfully place a story rather than trying to wedge it into a general program aimed at a broad audience.

"To me, this is an opportunity for companies to be even more customer focused and really be savvy about the specific audience to whom they want to sell their product or service," says Long. "It's an opportunity to be clear about your audience's likes and dislikes, how they want to get their information, and how to create loyalty and make them feel special."

A second trend is that broadcast, like print journalism, is becoming far more interactive. Increasingly, television stations are asking viewers to take opinion polls about top news issues and then broadcasting the results at the end of the newscast. They are also requesting viewers to provide information and footage related to the stories they report.

"There's now an opportunity for PR agencies to write good stories that get picked up," says Long. "There's lots of time to fill in a newscast, and if you have a great story or a great video, they're probably going to use it."

In addition, television and radio stations are archiving videocasts and podcasts on their Web sites, extending the shelf life of news. Increasingly, consumers are tuning in to a wide range of content after the fact from computer laptops, iPods, iPhones, and other devices. This makes it possible for a company to greatly increase the number of customers exposed to any story in which it is featured. You can archive broadcast stories about your company on your Web site, offering customers the opportunity to view or listen to them when and as often as they like.

When it comes to reaching out to your customers, it's important to keep in mind there's no single Holy Grail. Usually, various media are available for reaching your audience. The trick is to stay current on where your customers go for news and entertainment and continually identify the best paths with which to reach them.

LEVERAGE EMERGING TRENDS AND TECHNOLOGIES

When it comes to communicating, it's not just about print and broadcast anymore. Today 1.4 billion people worldwide—one of every five people on the planet—are using the Internet, according to Internet World Stats.[1] As the Internet comes of age, companies are increasingly turning to collaborative Web sites, blogs, podcasts, videocasts, social networks, virtual worlds, and other communication media to reach their audiences in innovative ways.

The Internet is changing the face of communication at a rapid clip. One day blogging is all the rage. The next day virtual worlds are the hot trend. To help their clients navigate the new world of interactive media, many PR firms are creating social media divisions and assigning vice presidents to lead them. More than half of PR firms that participated in a recent survey by the Council of Public Relations Firms currently have a dedicated interactive or digital group. What's more, nearly 80 percent of all PR firms say their existing and prospective clients are either "extremely interested" or "interested" in their firms' social media capabilities.[2]

As the Internet continues to usher in new ways of interacting with customers, it's important to keep your PR acumen current so you understand these communication tools and use them in the most strategic way possible. Mainstream publications are full of stories about Web technologies and their impact on business. Be curious and read everything you can about new communication media as they emerge. What demographic are they reaching? Are there any examples of companies that are using them effectively?

In addition, try out these communication media firsthand so you come to understand the culture. Sift through the top blogs and watch the top videos on YouTube. Work with your team to create your own blog or podcast. Develop a profile on one of the social networking sites. Using these tools yourself will give you a much clearer picture of how they are used and by whom. It may also generate some innovative ideas for how to target these media on behalf of your organization.

CONSUMER-GENERATED MEDIA

With the explosive growth of the Internet, consumers have more power than they've ever had before to influence the public perception of companies, their products, and services. Web sites such as Ratings.net and Epinions.com allow consumers to write reviews of everything from automobiles to electronics to video games. Web sites such as Amazon.com and Barnesandnoble.com include user reviews adjacent to the listing of each book, CD, and DVD they sell. Sites such as Yelp.com and TripAdvisor.com enable consumers to review restaurants, hotels, and professional services. Internet users are posting their opinions and personal experiences on a wide variety of message boards, discussion lists, wikis, and social networking sites. The amount of feedback consumers are providing is enormous.

Research has shown that consumers trust the opinions of other consumers more than they do those of traditional marketers and advertisers.[3] As a result, positive consumer opinions can tremendously boost a company's reputation and significantly multiply the number of customers. For example, Christopher Hall, owner of Splitends hair salon in Costa Mesa, California, says that Yelp is responsible for "tens over tens of thousands of dollars coming into my business." One of his customers wrote a Yelp review raving about her haircut, drawing many new customers to his salon. "They're all Yelpers," Hall told the *New York Times.* "They write reviews. It's speeding itself like a vacuum."[4]

On the other hand, scathing reviews or negative rumors spread about your organization, whether accurate or not, can seriously damage your company's reputation. As the consumer-generated media continues to dramatically alter the marketing landscape, it's important that companies develop a strategy for responding. (See sidebar, "Managing Your Online Reputation," on page 71.)

SEARCH ENGINE OPTIMIZATION

Today, when people want to know about a company's products and services, they typically turn to a search engine such as Google or Yahoo to do their research. If they "Google" your company, and there's little information, but there's ample information about your competitor, you're in a hole. "It's almost like instant brand reputation or brand reputation on demand," says Dennis Kaill, former president and managing director of Microscan Systems Inc. "If you're not investing in PR, it's a liability and detrimental to your organization. This is a big deal."

As the use of the Internet grows in sophistication, not only are companies archiving information on the Internet, the smart ones are trying to assert more control over their brands through search engine optimization (SEO). When a person keys in specific words using a search engine, the results are generated by computer programs that rank the Web pages in large part by examining the number and relative popularity of other sites that link to them.

SEO helps companies increase traffic to their Web site by improving the likelihood that popular keywords will turn up information about their company and do so high up in the rankings. "Anyone who looks for something on any search engine and thinks the results are the best or most impartial results, or that they came back completely organically is mistaken," search engine expert Danny Sullivan told the *New York Times*.[5]

Studies have shown that most people, when searching for information online, don't go beyond the first page of search results. "If it's not on the first page, it might as well be invisible," Sullivan says.[6] In an effort to boost their search rankings, many companies are conducting research to see what terms are typically keyed in by people whom they want to visit their site. They then ensure that these keywords are included in press releases, Web site copy, and other materials posted online. They're also learning linking techniques that will draw more readers to their Web site and are optimizing their video and images so they can be easily found through searches.

A popular example of the power of SEO was the success liberal bloggers had getting every major search engine to return George W. Bush's official White House biography every time a person typed in "miserable failure" into the search engine. (Conservative bloggers retaliated by pushing Jimmy Carter's official presidential biography to the No. 2 position and Hillary Rodham Clinton's Web site to the No. 5 position.)[7] While Google has since changed its overall algorithm to prevent such pranks from working, it demonstrates the power of SEO to associate people, companies, products, and services with specific keywords.

Building Awareness for Second Life

The following is an interview with Catherine Smith, director of marketing and brand strategy at Linden Lab. Second Life is the 3D digital online world created by Linden Lab.

Q: How do you approach PR with Second Life?

Catherine Smith: One of the things that's different about Second Life is the sheer volume of interest. I've never experienced anything like it before. At first I didn't do any proactive PR because I was completely immersed in responding to requests for information. My strategy today involves building a communications road map around the milestones of the company as well as the particular types of behaviors we wanted to encourage inside Second Life. And a lot of the PR I do is partnering with the "residents" of Second Life and what they do there. It's really about telling the stories of how residents are taking this environment and doing pretty amazing things in the areas of arts and culture, education, nonprofits, the open source community, and innovation.

Q: Why did you decide to focus your efforts on those particular areas?

Smith: Second Life is what it is because of the residents. It's all user-created content, and we feel some of the programs have been a wonderful use of the platform. For example, the education community in Second Life is rather large and exciting. At the same time, educators have a hard time getting funding for projects in Second Life as well as commitments from administrators. Our goal is to pull out these really great stories and make them more visible so educators can see their value while at the same time promoting the educational uses of Second Life.

Q: What are some of the other ways you've leveraged PR to generate awareness for Second Life?

Smith: When we were first formed, we hired an embedded reporter to report on the emerging community. His character was Hamlet Linden, and he was a game writer in the San Francisco area named W. James Au. James became the person who was reporting out of Second Life through his blog called New World Notes. His reports were an amazing way for us to learn about what was happening in Second Life and also to legitimize us without us being the people telling the stories. (He's not working for us anymore, but his blog still exists.)

At one point, players of the game World War II Online came into Second Life and ran everybody else out. They were pushing everyone else around, and they were attacked, and there was a protest. So there were some wonderful stories in New World Notes, especially during the first couple of years of Second Life, that told societal stories about this emerging culture.

Q: How did you get people to understand where his blog was?

Smith: James was very well-connected, so other blogs picked up what he was writing about. For instance, stories from New World Notes began appearing on Boing Boing, a technology and culture blog, and Terra Nova, which is a blog about virtual worlds. We weren't ready to go mainstream at the time. Our target audience was people who played multiple-player online games, and we tried to point these specific groups stories about Second Life to them. A lot of James's stories got picked up without our help. Interest in Second Life has been quite organic.

Q: When did Second Life really start to take off?

Smith: This is interesting. I had a friend who worked for Reuters and had breakfast with him and his wife in New York, and I told him about this new crazy place I was working. The whole idea of virtual land was so interesting to him that he called up and interviewed Philip Rosedale, the CEO of our company. When the story hit the wire, it just exploded. It got picked up everywhere, and the week culminated with Philip doing a live interview with CNN. That was in June 2004, about six months after Second Life was launched.

That's when things began to accelerate. By 2006, it was one story after another, and the hype just got louder and louder. And then it culminated in the fall of 2006 with Reuters entering Second Life and setting up a news bureau. We had 40,000 new residents sign up for Second Life in one day. We definitely felt like Second Life had suddenly come alive in a huge way.

Q: What role does PR currently play in the Linden Lab marketing mix?

Smith: It's the sole marketing tool we use. It works far better than advertising as a vehicle for telling the different ways people are using Second Life. For example, let's talk about someone who created an art installation in Second Life. Or let's talk about the single mom who's a fashion designer in Second Life bringing in money. Those are the kinds of stories that drive interest in Second Life as well as the behavior we're trying to encourage. We're interested in drawing new people who are going to come in and create more content.

Q: Are there any PR firms in Second Life?

Smith: Yes, there are hundreds, and I also believe there are resident-run firms. There are also at least twenty to thirty media outlets.

Q: Whom do they represent?

Smith: They represent other residents who have businesses and want to get some press. They're looking for both real-world press and in-world press. So if you have a new nightclub in Second Life, maybe you'd have a publicist and work with them to get the word out about your new club. And you'd take advantage of all the media outlets in the world in terms of buying advertising. Maybe you'd do an interview. Maybe you'd host a giant event. You need to get the word out, and you'd use the same tactics that you use in real life, basically.

Q: People have used Second Life to study behavioral patterns. Is there anything we can learn about the real world by observing the way media outlets interact with PR people in Second Life?

Smith: I think you can test new ideas and new campaigns in Second Life. The overhead is very little, which makes it possible to interact with residents in a way that's not possible in real life. Your universe is a lot smaller, but I think you have more access. On the flip side, a lot of people come in and try to do it just like they've done it in real life, and it doesn't work. It's not about putting up a banner ad. It's not about shouting out your message and expecting people to consume it. It's very different, and people who come in and try to do things the old-fashioned way often aren't successful. There's ample opportunity for exploration and experimentation, which is really fun.

THE WORLD OF BLOGGING

In the world of digital media, blogs are the most heavily leveraged medium. More than 19.4 million blogs are now active, with the size of the blogosphere doubling every six months, according to blog search engine Technorati.[8] These blogs are read by 110 million people worldwide, according to the Pew Internet & American Life Project report.[9]

Blogs are radically transforming the way information is created and disseminated, moving it from the previous centralized, top-down method into a more democratic process in which anyone can write about anything and potentially reach a large audience.

"Gone are the days when corporations could spend weeks obsessively crafting press releases and controlling their dissemination to the public," Larry Weber told *PRWeek*. "The blogosphere, e-communities, and social networks see right through the marketing-speak, tap into their own sources and instantly publish their unsanitized views to a global audience."[10]

In the new media landscape, any individual can quickly gain attention and become a respected "citizen journalist" by creating a blog. For example, the blog TVNewser, started by Towson University student Brian Stelter, whose previous experience was editing his college newspaper, has become widely regarded as required reading for high-powered television executives who want to keep up with the TV industry.[11] And the *Huffington Post*, the news and blog site started by Arianna Huffington, has quickly become one of the most widely read, linked to, and frequently cited media brands on the Internet.

As blogs grow in popularity, their influence on public perception is greatly increasing. According to a recent survey conducted by *PRWeek*, almost 60 percent of journalists say they use blogs to measure sentiment, almost 40 percent for finding subjects, and almost 30 percent for searching industry experts.[12] And Gannett News Service and other mainstream news organizations are officially changing their news-gathering policies to make better use of blogs.[13]

Companies can join the blogosphere in two ways. They can create their own blog to engage in a direct dialogue with customers, partners, and other stakeholders; or they can participate in the conversations taking place on existing blogs. To be considered a player, you need to raise your visibility in this space.

You also need to determine who's talking about your company's brand, products, and services and start to engage in dialogues to get your company exposed in as many of these places as possible.

Creating Your Own Blog

In recent years, a growing number of companies have developed their own blogs to deepen their relationships with key stakeholders and the public at large. For example, Google started a blog to present its perspective on controversial issues such as a copyright case involving insurance company GEICO and the Authors Guild's lawsuit to stop Google Print, which can search the text of books. Steve Langdon, Google's senior manager of corporate PR, told *PRWeek* that the blog enables Google to communicate with large numbers of people very quickly. "We would not announce earnings on the blog, but this was an appropriate use," he says.[14]

Sun Microsystems has also turned to blogging to shed itself of its corporate, blue-suit image. Using blogs, executives opened up the lines of communication to developers and users of Sun technology, allowing stakeholders to ask questions on any topic. Sun executives credit the direct interaction that blogging fosters with helping the company revive its brand.

"We had our share of bad news in the press, with people asking if the company was still viable," Sun Microsystem's chief marketing officer Anil Gadre told *PRWeek*. "But when we talked with customers face to face, they understood what we were doing and asked why we didn't tell this story to more people. But it's not a story you can tell just through ads or press releases. It's a story that also needs to be told through an unfiltered pipeline. The more touch points we have with our community, the more windows we have into the company's thinking."[15]

If your organization decides to create its own blog, make sure executives are willing to engage in honest debates about ideas rather than simply promoting the company product or service. It's also important to write the blog in conversational style, avoid jargon and marketing speak, and keep the blog up-to-date. Once you've created the blog, you can generate readership by e-mailing the link to key stakeholders, obtaining their permission to push new entries directly to their desktops, and encouraging other bloggers and partner Web sites to link to it.

Contributing to Existing Blogs

Whether or not you decide to create a blog for your company, you still need to monitor what other bloggers are saying about your company and the industry as a whole. With the vast number of blogs available, it's important to identify the most influential blogs in the category so you know which are the most important to reach. One easy way to gain an understanding of who's blogging about your company and your industry is to set up a Google Alert, which allows people to monitor news and blogs. Evaluate the quality of these posts, identify the reach of each blogger, and consider how much authority or credibility the blogger has.

After making a list of the blogs your company wants to reach, start reading them regularly and post responses when you have something to add to the discussion. Approaching bloggers is different than approaching journalists, and it won't work to send them a press release or a story pitch. Instead it's better to engage them in a conversation about something they have previously posted or post a direct response to their blog; this shows the bloggers you're reading their entries. You may want to invite some of the bloggers you've targeted to meet with you or others in your company. In addition, you should brief the bloggers you've identified in advance of your announcements and give them a heads-up on the news you're planning to announce.

When working with bloggers, it's important to fully disclose your identity and intentions and negotiate the ground rules in advance. If you want to embargo your news, for example, make sure the blogger knows what that means and has agreed to honor the embargo before you send over the news. To avoid potential employee conflicts, consider creating a company policy that outlines which employees can blog on behalf of your company and defines the parameters regarding what they can talk about. Keep in mind that the information people post on blogs is largely out of your control, but your company's power lies in its ability to respond and contribute to the dialogue. Blogs champion direct discourse and lively, open debates. If someone posts something negative about your company, you have the chance to respond. And if false information emerges about your company, you have the opportunity to set the record straight.

As with all social media, blogging is still very much an emerging medium, and companies are trying to determine how best to work with bloggers. The number of complex issues that have arisen as businesses enter into the world of blogging in 2007 led Coca-Cola, General Motors, SAP, Microsoft, and other leading companies to form the Blog Council. Among the major issues the Blog Council is planning to address are how to create responsible, ethical blogs; how to manage blogs in more than one language; and the correct way to engage bloggers who are writing about the company.

"Every major corporation is struggling with the question of how to use blogs and engage the blogosphere the right way," Sean O'Driscoll, general manager of community support services for Microsoft, said in a press release announcing the new council. "The Blog Council brings together precisely the people who need to explore these issues together, in a productive and private networking environment. We can work together to develop model policies that set the standard for corporate blogging excellence."[16]

Making the Most of Social Media

The following is an interview with Rick Murray, president of Edelman Digital.

Q: How do you define social media?

Rick Murray: Social media are the technologies that have evolved over the past five or ten years that are cheap, easy to use, and easy to access and that capture the latent demand of people at large to voice their opinions. The term "social media" is really kind of a misnomer. It's not a medium; it's not a transaction. It's a strategic tool to build relationships.

Q: How is the role of PR changing in the world of social media?

Murray: There's a demand for a different kind of relationship with your stakeholders. It's one that's focused on conversations, not campaigns; on dialogue, not monologue. It's about being flexible enough to adjust to the fact that people want information on demand. They want it where, when, how, wherever they happen to be, and in whatever form they want. With social media, our job as PR professionals is no longer to get a message out but rather to help companies build relationships with the people who are interested in them and who are interesting to them.

Q: Do you think companies today are fully embracing the opportunities that social media present?

Murray: Overall, I think companies recognize that social media is a vital part of the communications mix. But they tend to be at different places along the spectrum. At one end are those who believe it's a fad, and they're not paying attention to it at all. Further along the spectrum, some companies are listening to the conversation. They're paying attention to what's being said online, but they're not really doing anything about it. That's a great first step.

As they're moving a little further along, companies might be blogging to reach out to employees and setting up an internal social media policy that educates employees as to appropriate online behavior. A little further along, you might see companies participating in the online conversation in some low-risk ways. They might be putting some podcasts and videos out there, and posting some comments on blogs. And then as they get further down the line, they might start blogging, engaging in broad social networking activities, and thinking about how they can wrap all of this together.

Q: What are the risks of ignoring social media altogether?

Murray: Any company that's ignoring this today is going to lose significant market share within the next five years. Over time, they'll become less relevant to the people they should care about. It may not happen immediately and it may not happen on a huge scale right away, but over time if you're not participating in social media and your competitors are, your brand will come to be seen as less human, less caring, and less compassionate than those who are participating and are doing it right.

Q: How are the best companies making use of social media?

Murray: The companies that really get it are embedding social media into their operational strategy. They've fully embraced it and are using these technologies to build relationships with stakeholders. They're also thinking about the social aspect of communication, the need to communicate with people quickly, openly, honestly, transparently, fluidly, and in a way that embraces their flaws. They're admitting fault, and they're trying to help people out. Rather than saying in very prescriptive fashion, "This is what our business is about, and you need to understand," they're actually listening to the online conversation, they're engaging in dialogue, and they're doing it in real time in a very human way.

Q: Why are ethics and authenticity of the highest importance in the world of social media?

Murray: With social media, the rules of engagement are different. You're not a company, you're not a brand. You're a person, and you need to operate on a human level. The basis for any good relationship is honesty. To the extent that you violate that, you violate the trust that's inherent in the relationship. When I post a comment on a blog, it's not just Edelman talking. It's Rick Murray from Edelman. My personal reputation is at stake, my company's reputation is at stake, and those two are inextricably linked. Once you get that, it's very refreshing because nothing is scripted. If anything seems untrue or hyperbolic, you'll get called on it. Things need to be delivered in a very real and meaningful way.

Q: Can you provide some examples of companies that are leveraging social media effectively?

Murray: Comcast and Dell are both great examples. They are listening to the online conversations in near real time, and they're responding in near real time. Comcast has a person who watches the online conversation about Comcast on Twitter, and he responds in near real time. It you think about all the complaints you get in traditional call centers, listening and responding in near real time is an incredibly powerful tool. Basically you can turn detractors into fans and advocates literally overnight in one interaction.

Dell has created dellideastorm.com, which is essentially an online version of the old-fashioned suggestion box. People who care about Dell products post their ideas on the site, and the broader community reads all the suggestions and votes on the ones they think are important. To date, Dell has implemented well over 200 ideas that were submitted and voted on by the community. It's a great way for companies to reach out to customers to help them improve their products and services.

Q: What are some of the biggest pitfalls that you've seen companies fall into as they strive to embrace social media?

Murray: Some companies don't take it seriously, by which I mean they think they can work the way they've traditionally been working, and that's simply not the case. Some people treat social media like traditional media. They pitch stories without thinking about what's being said or how they're saying it, and that's generally a recipe for disaster.

Another pitfall is jumping in and out. The analogy I like to use is moving into the neighborhood. When you move into the neighborhood, you don't want to become known as the person who takes without giving back. In the same way, if you talk to a blogger or your community only when you have news you want to get out, you're not going to have a very productive or sustainable relationship. Companies that have moved from looking at social media from a transactional perspective to a relationship-building perspective are the ones seeing the best results.

Q: What advice do you have for companies that want to make better use of social media?

Murray: First of all, listen to the conversation. Take a look at what's being said about your company and the issues that affect it. While you're listening, put yourself in the average citizen's shoes. Don't think about it from an MBA perspective. Don't think that you can control it. Don't think that it can be another thing you can schedule and come in and out of.

Once you've listened, commit yourself to acting on the conversation. That means responding and engaging in a sustainable way. If the general tone and tenor of the conversations online is that your service is terrible or your products are inferior, just the fact that you're going up there and blogging about fixing things isn't enough if you don't actually fix them. Participation is absolutely important, but just listening and knowing what to do with the comments is the most important piece.

PODCASTS AND VIDEOCASTS

Podcasts and videocasts offer another, perhaps even more compelling, way to reach your audiences with finely targeted messages. The tipping point for videocasts came in February 2005 with the start of the video-sharing service YouTube; it came for podcasts shortly thereafter, in mid-2005, when Apple's newest version of iTunes began supporting the medium.

Today podcasts and videocasts are catching on, albeit at different speeds. Fifty-seven percent of online adults have used the Internet to watch or download a video, according to a study by the Pew Internet & American Life Project. About one in five do so on a typical day.[17] By comparison, the popularity of podcasts has been increasing more slowly. About 12 percent of Internet users have downloaded a podcast so they can listen to it at a later time while only 1 percent of Internet users report doing so on a typical day.[18]

As podcasts and videocasts attract a greater number of Internet users, companies are finding more ways to use these media to communicate with customers. General Motors uses podcasts to discuss the design of its cars and the auto races it sponsors. Virgin Atlantic Airways uses podcasts to provide customers with information about the destination cities to which it flies. And Walt Disney uses podcasts for everything from building awareness for its fiftieth anniversary to providing summertime tips for visiting the Disneyland resort.

Similarly, many organizations are raising awareness about their products and services through online videos and promotional contests via YouTube. For example, The March of Dimes educated the public about premature births and infant mortality by sponsoring a video contest in which people shared their personal stories. Home Depot sponsored a holiday video contest in which consumers were asked to detail the home improvement projects they would like to undertake. And Pizza Hut sought video submissions from consumers for its America's Favorite Pizza Fan Contest. In all three cases, the videos were uploaded onto YouTube, and the winner was judged by YouTube visitors. The organizations promoted the contests through blogs as well as press releases sent to traditional media outlets.

"We employ a wide variety of media and wanted to start incorporating this into our portfolio of media options," Manish Shrivastava, president of Home Depot Incentives told *PRWeek*. "It's a good way for us to learn and see what works for us in this space and optimize it from there."[19]

Podcasts and videocasts offer companies a way to create buzz without spending a great deal of money. When creating them, however, it's critical that the information you highlight is informative and entertaining rather than self-promotional. If you work for a company that sells a diet product, for example, create a podcast or video about the challenges of overcoming obesity, not about your product. Better yet, have some of your customers talk directly about their personal challenges fighting obesity.

The content must be interesting and authentic if you want people to watch the video all the way through. It's also important to keep it short. You can attract people to your podcasts and videocasts by posting them on your organization's Web site, embedding them in blogs, and posting them on YouTube or one of the many smaller online video sites and including text on the page to make them searchable. To make sure your podcast or videocast resonates with your intended audience, test it with focus groups before releasing it more broadly. In addition, create a feedback mechanism so you can measure the response and fine-tune your podcasts and videocasts over time.

SOCIAL NETWORKING SITES

Social networks, in which users post personal profiles, upload photos and videos, and interact with other individuals, have exploded in popularity in recent years. According to one survey, 45 percent of all active Web users are using social networking sites.[20]

The two leading social networks, MySpace and Facebook, were launched in 2003 and 2004 and now host more than 110 million and 60 million users respectively.[21] To date, both sites have mainly been used as a tool for connecting with friends and building relationships. Increasingly, however, companies are getting in on the scene, testing ways to use these sites as marketing tools. Since 2007, when Facebook began allowing corporate profiles, numerous businesses have developed a presence on the site. For example, Verizon posted a profile that includes its Web site link, company overview, product reviews, sample ring tones, product photos, and videos. Blockbuster also has a Facebook profile that showcases its latest movie releases, special offers, and Movie Clique, a widget that lets users rate movies and suggest must-see films to friends.

With the debut of Facebook Ads, users can now use the social network to recommend products to friends. In addition, some organizations have started taking advantage of a polling feature that lets Facebook users post a question and target it to users based on gender, age, location, or profile keyword. Since Facebook decided to make its code available to third-party developers, some companies have also turned to the site as their primary vehicle for launching and promoting new applications. For example, iLike, a music discovery service that allows users to discover and share music playlists, halted work on its own Web site in order to promote its application on Facebook. Although a risky move, it has apparently paid off. Within the first twelve hours, iLike signed up more than 10,000 users through Facebook,[22] and use of the application continues to expand.

Managing Your Online Reputation

As an increasing number of consumers venture online to post opinions about companies, products, and services, it's more important than ever to build a solid online reputation. Here are some tips for maintaining a good reputation in the new world of consumer-generated media:

1. Monitor what people are saying. Read blogs that follow your industry. Set up a Google Alert to notify you when your organization or key people are mentioned online. Use free tools such as BlogPatrol and Technorati to monitor what people are saying about your organization and who is reading the content you post. Type the company name in the major search engines to see what comes up. The first step toward developing a solid reputation is understanding how people currently view your organization.

2. Proactively create content about your organization. Consider starting a company blog. Establish your organization as an authority by contributing to outside forums, blogs, and news sites. Create positive online content about your organization on Facebook, MySpace, LinkedIn, and other social networking sites. Use search engine optimization techniques to ensure that keywords are associated with your company when people search online.

3. Weigh the consequences before responding to a negative comment. If a person posts a negative comment about your company or product, carefully weigh whether a response is warranted. How many readers will see the comment? Will a response just fuel the fire, or is it truly needed to set the record straight? By replying to every negative comment regardless of reach or import, you risk intensifying the problem by building more negative content for people to see.

4. Always be honest. If a response is warranted, always reply honestly. Admit your mistakes, and explain what you've done to rectify the issue. Similarly, never respond in a way that's personal or defensive. Always take the high road.

5. Resolve issues offline. If someone had a negative experience with your product or service, try to resolve the situation one-on-one by taking the discussion offline. Determine if the person is willing to provide you with an e-mail address or phone number, and then contact her directly to work out a solution. Who knows, the person may be so impressed with your response that she follows up with a positive post discussing your prompt attention to the issue.

6. Rally support from your friends. While one person may have had a negative experience with your product, far more may think the product is top-notch. Encourage your customers, clients, and other allies to share their experiences online.

7. Request removal of incorrect information. If someone makes a comment that is blatantly wrong or slanderous, contact the owner of the blog, forum, or news site and ask that the comment be removed. If the owner refuses, consider hiring a lawyer. Alternatively, ask the Web site owner to publish your response and issue a statement on your Web site.

VIRTUAL WORLDS

Virtual worlds have also opened up opportunities for companies wanting to promote their brands. For example, many organizations are finding ways to engage "residents" of Second Life, a 3D virtual world populated by millions of people who interact in the form of avatars. In October 2006, Sun Microsystems became the first Fortune 500 company to hold a press conference in Second Life. The event was hosted by Sun Chief Researcher John Gage, who appeared in avatar form, and marked the kickoff of Sun's Project Darkstar, designed to help developers of online games with server-side technology.

"Second Life is creating new possibilities for communication, sharing, and community building, all principles which have guided Sun since its founding," Gage said during the press conference. "Second Life is a community built entirely on participation, and, while this is still an experiment for us, we're jumping into Second Life with both feet because we see the online world's unlimited potential for collaboration on everything from social issues to Java technology development."[23]

Coca-Cola also has also taken advantage of virtual worlds, entering Second Life by issuing an invitation to residents to submit ideas for a portable virtual Coca-Cola vending machine. Car manufacturer Nissan marketed its new Sentra on Second Life by creating a driving course on Sentra Island, letting users test out the new models in 3D fashion. Similarly, Toyota took its youth-targeted Scion brand into Second Life, giving away virtual vehicles to launch its presence there. At the time, Toyota's marketing manager, Adrian Si, told the *Economist* that Toyota hoped Second Life residents would customize the cars so Toyota could obtain customer insights into improvements it should make to the real-world vehicle.[24]

"I think you can test campaigns inside of Second Life, and you can test new ideas," says Catherine Smith, director of marketing and brand strategy for Linden Lab, the creator of Second Life. "Of course, your universe is a lot smaller than in the real world, but I think you have a lot more access. There's ample opportunity for exploration and experimentation, which is really fun."

EMBRACING SOCIAL MEDIA OPPORTUNITIES

So how should your company go about evaluating social media opportunities to make sure they're right for its business? And how can you participate in this new arena in a way that advances, rather than harms, your brand? Here are eight rules for successfully navigating the Web landscape:

1. *Keep up with emerging trends and technologies.* The Internet is evolving at lightning speed, so it's important to stay knowledgeable about current trends. Read everything you can so you know what's coming down

the pike. In addition, try out new Web technologies yourself so you develop a clear understanding of how they're used. "I liken it to doing business in a foreign country," Simple Star CEO Chad Richard, a user of MySpace, told *PRWeek*. "You need to visit, understand the cultural nuances, and see for yourself, instead of just reading industry reports."[25]

2. *Understand who's using the medium.* Before establishing an organizational presence, it's critical that you research each medium in advance so you understand the exact audience it reaches. For example, Facebook, which began as a social networking site for college students, draws nearly half of its audience from visitors aged twenty-four and younger, according to digital media measurement group comScore. By comparison, visitors to MySpace generally skew older, with people twenty-five and older comprising 68 percent of its user base.[26] Knowing just this one piece of information will help you choose the better medium, depending on the age group you seek to reach. Keep in mind the demographics for each of these social media outlets continue to evolve rapidly as more people join them. As a result, it's important to constantly update your research so you continue to focus your efforts in the right places over time.

3. *Know your business objectives.* As with any public relations initiative, it's critical that any venture into the world of social media be tied to your broader business objectives. Developing a YouTube video may be trendy, but it will have no impact unless it advances your organizational goals. Deloitte's effort to launch the Deloitte Film Festival was successful because the company used the initiative to achieve two very clear goals: attract more Generation Y job candidates and engage its existing workforce in a fun, creative way. As part of the initiative, Deloitte invited all of its employees to produce short films that capture the organization's culture and values. The films were posted on an internal YouTube-like intranet site, where they were rated by Deloitte employees, with the best ones integrated into Deloitte's campus recruiting programs.

   "We were specifically trying to build eminence for Deloitte and raise visibility in the recruiting space," says Keith Lindenburg, director, national public relations, Deloitte Services LP. "We're hiring thousands of people every year in a highly competitive market, and we were looking for ways to help us stand out."

4. *Stick to your promises.* If you're considering a contest, make sure you clearly describe the rules upfront and then stick to them all the way through your campaign. For example, the Malibu brand took a hit on YouTube after the company launched a video contest soliciting ads

for its Malibu Banana Rum. The company said it would consider the votes of YouTube users when selecting a winner, yet the finalists were never publicly named. The situation created an uproar on YouTube, with some of the consumers who lost the contest posting accusations on YouTube message boards saying that the contest had been rigged. The *New York Times* also eventually picked up the story, causing further damage to the Malibu brand.[27]

5. *Anticipate what could go wrong.* Social media, by definition, is a place for spontaneous and uncontrolled dialogue. Therefore, it's important to consider the viability of your campaign before you roll it out, brainstorming all of the unanticipated directions in which people might take it. Take Chevrolet, for example. The company introduced a Web site allowing visitors to take existing video clips and insert their own words to create a customized thirty-second commercial for the 2007 Chevrolet Tahoe. The hope was that Internet users would e-mail their own videos around the Web, generating interest for the Tahoe. What ended up happening instead was that some people developed videos critical of the SUV and its low gas mileage, and these videos became the ones most widely circulated around the Web.[28]

   "Social media can be a double-edged sword," says Brad Stevens, former vice president of U.S. marketing for Starbucks. "There's a lot of anti-corporate sentiment in much of that area of the Web, so you really have to be careful about how you use it."

6. *Be upfront about your identity.* Whole Foods learned the importance of revealing your identity the hard way. CEO John Mackey was accused of attempting to manipulate stocks and misleading investors after he anonymously posted numerous messages to a Yahoo Finance board attacking Wild Oats while cheering on his own company at a time when his company was trying to purchase Wild Oats. The Federal Trade Commission brought the incident to light in a lawsuit seeking to block the Wild Oats takeover on antitrust grounds, triggering a slew of bad press for Whole Foods.[29] As a general rule, never post anything anonymously in the online community. If you can't be transparent about what you're doing, simply don't do it.

7. *Disclose your company's agenda.* Again, don't be secretive. If your company is sponsoring a particular effort, you need to state that upfront. The public relations agency Edelman was forced to apologize publicly after the firm and its client Wal-Mart failed to disclose they were behind the blog walmartingacrossamerica.com. The blog, which chronicled a couple's journey across the United States in an RV while stopping at Wal-Mart parking lots, appeared to be a grassroots effort.

Yet it turns out it was funded by Working Families for Wal-Mart, a Wal-Mart-backed organization developed to promote a positive image of the company.[30] "Companies that attempt to deceive consumers run the risk of a back lash and generating negative word of mouth," writes the Word of Mouth Marketing Association. "So whether it's blogs, or mystery shoppers or promotions disguised as market research, it's better to be upfront and let your audience know what the real purpose is, they're smart enough to tell."[31]

8. *Fight fairly.* Even if you're treated unfairly, always be above board in the way you respond. Microsoft wanted to change incorrect information posted on Wikipedia but was barred by a Wikipedia policy that prevents public relations professionals, campaign workers, and others with a perceived conflict of interest from editing entries on its online encyclopedia. To get around this requirement, Microsoft secretly paid an Australian blogger to edit the article, triggering a debate about the ethics of the company's behavior in the blogging community.[32] If blogs are going to be the great equalizer, we believe no one should be barred from editing sites such as Wikipedia. Still, it would have been better if Microsoft addressed the situation directly—by blogging about the unfairness of the situation on its own site, for example—rather than covertly hiring a blogger to make the corrections.

As the Internet comes of age, public relations is becoming an increasingly exciting field. The possibilities abound for reaching your customers in new and creative ways. Approaching these opportunities in a thoughtful and ethical manner will enable your organization to form deeper relationships with your audiences by engaging directly with them without a filter. It will also help ensure that you foster strong relationships while building an inspiring brand over time.

DEVELOP A STRATEGIC PR PLAN

If you have any doubt just how important a PR plan is, look no further than to Cynthia McKay. Hoping to increase sales for her small gourmet gift company in Castle Rock, Colorado, she hired a PR firm that took her money without telling her what it would achieve on her behalf. Three weeks and $3,000 later, there were no results.

Her experience wasn't much better after she eventually turned to a pay-per-placement PR firm. The firm pitched stories without engaging in strategy development, failing to outline in advance which media outlets it would pitch and how these story placements would contribute to her overall business goals. McKay was initially charged $2,500 for placement in a cover story about careers in a well-known women's magazine. Later she was billed $11,000 for a mention in the Associated Press about her company's gift basket donations to soldiers in Iraq. The PR firm charged her every time a different newspaper picked up the story. Not surprisingly, McKay ended up feeling "nickel and dimed," as she told the *Wall Street Journal*.[1]

Often companies hire PR firms without understanding what the results or the costs will be. Regardless of whether they work with an internal PR staff or hire an outside firm, companies must understand the value and the cost of their PR efforts before they get started. The best way to do that is to outline all the pieces in a compelling PR plan.

RALLYING THE TROOPS

A detailed PR plan helps ensure that everyone is moving in the same direction. It helps to rally the troops around a common goal. We recently watched the 100th Apple Cup, the annual football game between the University of Washington Huskies and Washington State University Cougars, the two largest universities in the state of Washington. Sadly, the Huskies lost the game on the final play because half of the players ran one play while the other half ran another. It was an embarrassing moment. No common game plan had been in place, and it cost them the game. "We just blew the coverage," said University of Washington coach Tyrone Willingham after the game. "Our communication was not good, not complete across the board. We had some guys playing one thing and some playing something else."[2]

Without a PR plan, a company risks the same disaster. The result may be that half of its employees move in one direction, and the other half in another, unknowingly undermining the work of the first half. To help ensure that everyone is united and moving in the same direction, it's essential that companies operate from a common PR plan. By developing a strategic plan, companies stay focused on achieving their most important goals without getting distracted or sidetracked. "I think having a good plan is really important because it guards against unrealistic expectations," says Lee Weinstein, principal of Lee Weinstein & Associates and the former director of global corporate communications for Nike. "It allows you to come back later and say, 'Here's what we said we were going to do, here's what we did, and here's how you can evaluate against it.'"

Like a detailed architectural blueprint, a PR plan helps everyone get in sync as to what's going to be accomplished over what time frame and for what cost. It sets expectations and prevents unwanted surprises, making it an essential tool for companies of all sizes. A PR plan becomes even more critical for large companies with hundreds of employees or complex initiatives that involve many players. When Apple launched the iPhone, for example, it worked with hundreds of partners ranging from wireless operators to software developers. Can you imagine the chaos that would have ensued had all these partners failed to work from a common PR plan? They would have all operated in discord, clumsily bumping into one another as they touted conflicting messages.

CHARACTERISTICS OF A SUCCESSFUL PR PLAN

So what exactly makes a PR plan compelling? First, it needs to be thoroughly *researched*. It should convey a clear understanding of your company's business objectives. If you haven't done so already, spend some time answering the list of questions in "The Case for a Strategic Approach to PR," designed to help you identify your organization's business objectives and what you want PR to help you achieve. Every successful PR plan includes an up-to-date description of the current market situation, the latest marketplace trends, and the company's position as compared with its industry competitors. Gathering and synthesizing this information in a thorough and thoughtful manner takes time and requires a good deal of critical thinking.

Second, a compelling PR plan is tightly *focused*. Every effort outlined in the PR plan should help your company achieve its most important business objectives. Where is your organization today, and where do you want it to be tomorrow? Once you determine the direction, every effort you engage in should either move you toward it or be discarded.

Third, a compelling PR plan is *creative*. PR professionals often try to take shortcuts by reapplying the same efforts that worked for another PR campaign or client, the approach being that a press release worked in that situation, so let's just reapply it to the PR campaign we're working on now. The problem with this approach is that it fails to focus on the true business problems of the particular client or situation in front of you. Every PR campaign is different and deserves its own creative thinking.

Fourth, a compelling PR plan should be *integrated* and support the efforts of other departments in the organization. Is it in harmony with the goals of the marketing department and the sales department and the overall business goals of the company? Make sure you examine any other plans that exist so that the PR plan is in sync. If the PR plan conflicts with any other functional group within the organization, either it should be changed or a meeting with all the key players should be held so everyone is brought into sync as to the high-level goals of the company.

Fifth, a compelling PR plan should be *holistic*. It takes into consideration your company's entire news cycle and maintains momentum between major announcements. Too often, companies let the momentum subside between major announcements, losing the visibility they've worked so hard to create. With a little planning, it's possible to continue the momentum so that you don't lose mindshare among the media or customers between major initiatives.

Finally, a compelling PR plan is *realistic*. By that we mean that all the strategies and tactics outlined in the PR plan can be accomplished within the available budget and time frame. If you have only $20,000 per month to work with, make sure the strategies and tactics you outline can be accomplished within this budget. If you have only a couple of months leading up to the launch of a product, make sure all the publications you work with are able to publish your story within this time frame.

Realistic also means that all the strategies and tactics are achievable. Let's say your strategy is to win the football game by scoring a touchdown at the end of the fourth quarter, and to do that, one of your tactics is to throw an eighty-yard pass at the end of the fourth quarter. The chance of completing the pass is really low, which probably makes it a flawed approach. In the same way, you can come up with the most creative strategies and tactics, but if they can't be realistically achieved, they aren't worth their salt and should be rejected. As Al Ries and Jack Trout write in their book *Marketing Warfare,* "A grand strategy can be awesome, inspirational, audacious, and bold, yet an utter failure if it doesn't put troops in the field in exactly the right place and at the right time to accomplish the job tactically."[3]

THE BALL PARK PR PLAN

One of our all-time favorite PR programs was a campaign developed by Sara Lee to raise awareness for its Ball Park hot dog brand. The goal was to keep the Ball Park brand front and center during the summer months, when barbecuing is at its height. To accomplish this, Ball Park created a contest showcasing the best hot dog toppings consumers could come up with. The Great American Hot Dog Taste Challenge invited consumers in nine markets that Ball Park wanted to dominate to bring recipes that spoke to the traditions of their respective cities. Ball Park generated participation in the contests by pitching media stories in advance of each city event. After the contest was over, chefs from Sara Lee appeared on local morning shows to demonstrate recipes from local winners.

Altogether, 41,000 people attended contest events across the United States, sampling more than 15,000 hot dogs. By the time the contest ended, traffic to Sara Lee's Web site had increased 30 percent. "It exceeded our expectations," Sara Matheu, director of media development and communications at Sara Lee, told *PRWeek.* "We really feel like we have 41,000 new brand ambassadors out there."[4]

This is a great example of a PR campaign because it's *creative, focused,* and *integrated* with Sara Lee's overall goals for the Ball Park brand. The company found an innovative way to accomplish its goal of building awareness of its brand—by holding a contest that encouraged thousands of consumers to taste its hot dogs—and then highlighting the winners on morning television shows watched by millions. At the same time, the contest was tightly focused. It didn't target all consumers. Instead it focused on nine specific markets Ball Park was trying to dominate. What's more, neither the campaign nor the editorial coverage that accompanied it was initiated simply for the sake of doing PR. The effort was tied to an important business objective: increasing sales of Ball Park hot dogs.

Ways to Spark Your Creativity

After you've worked in public relations for a while, it's easy to slip into a rut and continually implement the same tactics that have worked in the past without exploring new ideas. As a result, PR campaigns can become stale. To get the best results, every PR plan should involve its own fresh thinking and implement the best creative ideas. So what can you do to start thinking more creatively? Here are seven tips:

- *Warm up your creative juices.* A great way to loosen up your thinking is to complete some warm-up exercises. Try writing down everything that pops into your head, stream-of-consciousness style, for five minutes, keeping your pen moving the whole time. Or open a magazine to a random page and let your mind free-associate with the image on the page, writing down everything it reminds you of. Once you've loosened up your mind, begin brainstorming ideas for your PR plan.

- *Try mind mapping.* Mind mapping is a technique that helps people see new relationships and possibilities through the use of diagrams. Write down a word or idea in the middle of the page, and draw a circle around it. Next to that idea, write down words you associate with it, drawing a circle around each word you write. Eventually you'll have a non-linear page filled with ideas for your PR plan.

- *Organize a group brainstorming session.* Group brainstorming is a great way to explore new ideas. Assemble your team in a room, ask a question, and then write down everyone's ideas on a whiteboard, without judgment. After all the ideas are out there, revisit them as a group to pick out the best possibilities.

- *Take a walk.* Take a twenty-minute walk, trying to think of ideas while away from the office. Or better yet, go for a brainstorming walk with a coworker. It's amazing how we generate some of our best ideas when we remove ourselves from the situation.

- *Keep a PR notebook.* Read as much as you can about other industries, companies, and PR campaigns; and keep a notebook containing ideas and approaches that inspire you. You can also use your notebook to jot down your own ideas and to take notes as you read.

- *Bounce your ideas off another person.* Come up with some initial ideas, and then bounce them off a coworker, a friend, or your spouse. Great solutions can unexpectedly pop into your head if you describe the problem out loud.

- *Enroll in a creativity class.* Numerous books and classes are available that are designed to help people unleash their creativity; many of them include hands-on exercises. Read about creativity or enroll in a class, then regularly practice what you learn.

THE BRAINSTORM PROCESS

So how do you go about developing a PR plan? First, determine the length of time it should cover. Companies typically operate from a twelve-month PR plan that incorporates their overarching goals for the year and gives them a high-level view into what they want to accomplish. In addition, they often create mini-PR plans that serve as a more detailed road map for specific product launches and other significant announcements slated to occur during the course of the year.

Once you've figured out the timeline, schedule a brainstorm session to capture the creative thinking of the group. This session should include as many types of people as possible, especially those who might be a consumer of the particular product or service you're trying to promote. If you work inside a company, consider including employees in different parts of the organization, and even colleagues outside the company, who aren't working on your particular announcement. If you're employed at a PR agency, include colleagues who aren't working on your account. Our experience has shown that by the time the brainstorm session is scheduled, employees working on the account often have already started to form a point of view based on their initial research or discussions. Opening up the brainstorm session to a broader spectrum of people encourages a fresh perspective and a wider range of ideas.

We typically begin the brainstorm session by providing an overview of the business and communication objectives we want to achieve and the audiences we want to reach and then asking the group to help us develop some of the strategies and tactics that will help to accomplish these objectives. To come up with the best strategies and tactics, you may want to pose some of these high-level questions:

- Where are customers' minds today? Where do we want their minds to be tomorrow?
- How do we need to position our company? What are the best ways to do that?
- What role can third parties (customers, analysts, partners) play to help tell our story?
- What kind of competitive response can we anticipate?
- What events might we leverage to help us achieve our objectives?
- What announcements should we plan for during the time period of the PR plan?
- What are we going to do to maintain momentum when we have no news?
- Are there trends we can leverage to tell our story?
- What colorful detail exists (interesting personalities, experiences, graphics, visuals, statistics) that will help us bring our story to life?
- How will we measure success?

Once you answer these questions, it will become clearer what strategies and tactics are needed to help you meet your objectives. Using a whiteboard, we list all of the suggestions without any judgment as to whether each is a good or bad idea. After the brainstorm session is over, the team working on the PR plan evaluates the ideas, incorporating the best ones into the plan. This approach ensures that we come up with the widest range of creative ideas. It also prevents us from taking a cookie-cutter approach, in which we recycle the same ideas over and over again.

"When I do PR planning, one of the things I like to do is talk about what would nirvana be if we executed this campaign with perfection," Weinstein says. "Do we want our story to be in the *New York Times* Style section? Do we want MTV news to cover it? We then build our plan back from that and make sure it syncs up with our budget, brand, and mission. That allows us to be really strategic."

THE BUILDING BLOCKS OF A STRATEGIC PLAN

Whether you're working on an overarching PR plan or a miniplan, a strategic plan always has most or all of the following ten components. Like a series of interlocking LEGOs, each section should build upon the one that comes before it, starting with a situation analysis and ending with a conclusion:

1. *Situation analysis*
    The situation analysis is like the president's state of the union address. It should discuss the state of affairs for the industry as well as the company itself. It should also describe the competitive marketplace as well as any legislative issues and trends that are affecting the industry. The purpose of the situation analysis is to ensure that all participants are operating from the same assumptions so there's consensus as to how to move forward.

    We developed the following situation analysis as part of an overall PR plan for a fictitious company, Hunsk Motorcycles.[5] The entire PR plan, included in the Appendix, demonstrates the creative thinking that a good strategic PR plan should include.

    *   Hunsk Motorcycles has been in business for more than twenty years. Its main competitor is Harley-Davidson.
    *   Hunsk customers are primarily men aged thirty-five to fifty and college educated who view themselves as risk-takers. They want a bike that "ticks like a clock and moves like a rocket."
    *   Through the first six months of this year, shipments of Hunsk motorcycles were approximately 125,900 units, a 7.2 percent decrease compared to last year's 135,600 units.

- The company anticipates that U.S. economic conditions and ongoing consumer concerns will continue to create challenges at least through the end of the year. Nonetheless, the executive management team remains confident about its future and is committed to managing and reinvesting in the business for the long term.
- The management team recognizes that the Hunsk marketing campaign, with its ineffective materials and positioning, is outdated; it's lost its "oomph." The PR and marketing campaigns are not reaching the company's target audience, and the employees promoting its motorcycles don't always have direct experience with the product.
- In the past, Hunsk has updated its marketing campaigns to align with trends in the broader consumer market (younger demographic, eco-friendly business practices, lightweight body and machinery) and in the process has lost touch with its core demographic, neglecting to establish a key message and value proposition that resonated with its customer base.
- The company is interested in getting back to its marketing roots, with a goal to be more authentic. Again, the company's core demographic is men who view themselves as the real rebels. They are fiercely independent, confident, and edgy.

2. *Business objectives*
   The business objective section offers a statement about what the organization as a whole is trying to achieve. Perhaps your business objective is to build the perceived value of the company or to broaden your customer base by moving into a new geographical area of the country.

   We created the following three business objectives for Hunsk Motorcycles:

   - Boost sales and drive revenue.
   - Reconnect with the core customer and recapture market share from competitors.
   - Build the perceived value of the company.

3. *Target audiences*
   This section should provide a list of the key audiences you want to reach to meet your business goals. For example, Hunsk Motorcycles wants to target four audiences:

   - Consumers, primarily men aged thirty-five to fifty
   - Employees
   - Shareholders
   - Investors

4. *Communication objectives*

The communications objectives section outlines your broad communications goals for each of the target audiences you are planning to reach. It should clearly state the desired perceptions of your company by the end of the time period covered by the PR plan.

For Hunsk Motorcycles, we developed three communications objectives:

- Elevate the visibility and value of the brand.
- Deepen relationships with loyal customers and enthusiasts.
- Create a sustainable platform for coverage across a variety of media, positioning Hunsk as the maker of the finest motorcycles in the world.

5. *Key messages*

This section lays out the key messages you want to communicate to each audience. To develop these messages, consider specific messages for each audience to adopt the specific perception you seek. You may want to develop one set of messages for your company and another set of messages for each product or service. Each message should be simple, powerful, and descriptive.

We crafted the following key messages for Hunsk Motorcycles:

- Hunsk is in the business of making the world's best motorcycles to create exceptional experiences for its customers. The company is committed to innovation as it continues producing great motorcycles.
- The company has the right management team in place and is well poised to position Hunsk for the future, to strengthen its bonds with its current customers, and to secure new customers. The road ahead is looking bright.
- Outstanding corporate governance has been a long-standing business practice at Hunsk because it makes good business sense. Although the motorcycle business is fun, corporate governance is something we take seriously.
- Hunsk understands that its customers don't want to be sold to. They want to be part of the brand and what it represents, which is the freedom, excitement, and adventure of the open road.

6. *Strategy and tactics*

Every PR plan should present a strategy overview that collectively discusses all the strategies you plan to implement to bring your communication objectives to fruition and why you chose them. Here is the strategy overview we drafted for Hunsk Motorcycles:

We have identified the following six strategies that Communiqué PR can implement on behalf of Hunsk Motorcycles. These strategies can be executed in tandem or as disparate projects.

Strategy 1: Demonstrate Hunsk's value with motorcycle enthusiasts.
Strategy 2: Tie Hunsk to key lifestyle trends and consumer habits.
Strategy 3: Tell the story of Hunsk's reinvention and return to its roots.
Strategy 4: Create support for Hunsk online.
Strategy 5: Hit the road with museum participation.
Strategy 6: Pursue and win industry awards.

Each strategy should be given its own section that includes a description of the strategy and the tactics required to accomplish it. Here's a description of the first of the six strategies for Hunsk Motorcycles as well as the tactics we identified:

Strategy 1: Demonstrate Hunsk's value with motorcycle enthusiasts.

To help Hunsk Motorcycles reach its target audience and demonstrate value to them, we recommend placing articles in the magazines read by serious motorcycle enthusiasts. Specifically, we envision targeting journalists with *American Motorcyclist*, *Easyriders*, *Rider*, and others for coverage. Communiqué PR would reach out to editors of these magazines with the goal of reviving awareness of the brand and securing coverage about Hunsk. In the coming quarter, we anticipate spending seventy hours on this strategy.

Tactics

- Determine angle and messages for a pitch to motorcycle enthusiast publications. We believe the following story angles would resonate with the readers of these publications:

  o "Tips for Taking a Tour on Your Hunsk." Five tips highlighting reasons that Hunsk bikes can make your road trip the best ever. (Includes list of top Hunsk accessories and recommended routes.)
  o "Maintenance Tips from the Pros for Bikers." Position Hunsk as a subject matter expert on what bikers need most or how Hunsk owners can fix and tune up their own bikes.
  o "Riding Free, Riding Safe: Tips to Keep You on the Road." Focus on ways that riders can maintain their freedom and stay safe.

- Develop first-draft pitch materials.
- Review materials with Hunsk executives.
- Develop second-draft pitch materials.
- Work with Hunsk vice president of marketing to secure final approvals on all materials.
- Distribute pitches and story suggestions to journalists.
- Follow up with a round of phone calls to spark journalists' interest in writing about Hunsk.
- Place a second round of phone calls.
- Recap results from discussions with journalists.
- Facilitate interviews (assuming we'll secure three to five interviews for Hunsk executives with these magazines).
- Develop recap of calls.
- Work with the journalists to ensure they have artwork to accompany the story.

7. *Budget*

Here you'll want to describe the overall budget as well as the number of hours per month it will take to implement the entire plan. If you're working with a tight budget, you may want to get even more detailed by providing the estimated cost of each strategy and tactic. This helps to prioritize opportunities, enabling your organization to focus on the efforts most critical to the campaign. It also makes it easier to negotiate additional budget should company executives want to add more strategies and tactics to the plan. For example:

Strategy	Hours	Rate	Fees
Demonstrate Hunsk's value with motorcycle enthusiasts	70	$200	$14,000
Tie Hunsk to key lifestyle trends and consumer habits	140	$200	$28,000
Tell the story of Hunsk's reinvention and return to its roots	100	$200	$20,000
Create support for Hunsk online	180	$200	$36,000
Hit the road with museum participation	500	$200	$100,000
Pursue and win industry awards	120	$200	$24,000
Total			**$222,000**

8. *Timeline*

To establish accountability, the PR plan should include a timeline that outlines projected accomplishments within a specific period of time. The timeline should also describe who will be executing which part of the plan. That way there's no confusion about who's responsible for each effort when you later go back and review the plan's success:

Strategy	Timeline
Demonstrate Hunsk's value with motorcycle enthusiasts.	Q3
Tie Hunsk to key lifestyle trends and consumer habits.	Q4
Tell the story of Hunsk's reinvention and return to its roots.	Q4
Create support for Hunsk online.	Ongoing
Hit the road with museum participation.	Ongoing
Pursue and win industry awards.	Ongoing

9. *Measurements of success*

This section is extremely important because it creates shared expectations as to the nature of a successful campaign. Success can be measured in many ways, which we will discuss in detail in Principle 9. Whether you're measuring success by the number of story placements, the quality of comments, or the cost per impression, it's important to outline these measurements in as much detail as possible. This allows you to revisit the plan at the end of the campaign to determine whether it was moderately successful, wildly successful, or less successful than you had hoped. It also eliminates the risk that different executives within the company will develop different sets of expectations regarding success. The following are two measurements of success we developed for the first strategy of the Hunsk Motorcycles PR plan:

- Build relationships with ten journalists with magazines written for motorcycle enthusiasts.
- Secure three positive articles about Hunsk and its bikes.

10. *Conclusion*

The conclusion provides an opportunity to discuss any parting thoughts and ask company executives for their input. Here's the conclusion we drafted for our Hunsk Motorcycles PR plan:

We are eager to receive your feedback on this plan and hope it provides a detailed road map of our proposed activity. Please feel free to contact me with any questions. I may be reached at name@communiquepr.com or at (555) 555-5555, ext. 123.

CRAFT A COMPELLING STORY

With 200 pounds on his five-foot-four-inch frame, Brad Hefta-Gaub was a self-described couch potato who sat around at home and ate lots of junk food. Facing the onset of poor health and disease, he decided it was time to get healthy. He took up running, biking, and swimming, eventually reducing his weight to 140 pounds and cutting his body fat nearly in half, from 36 percent to 19 percent.

Now a marathon runner and Ironman triathlete, the former RealNetworks and Revenue Science executive and his partner Phil Sabin have rolled out an online social network called Sweat365.com. The Web site helps athletes of all levels track their daily routines, find competitive events, and interact with others who share similar workout goals. Americans now spend $60 billion a year on diet and fitness programs. With one-third of American adults obese and two-thirds overweight, there's clearly a need for long-term fitness solutions that work. Sweat365.com is the first social network to support people in the common goal of becoming more fit.

"Our goal is to motivate and inspire people to change their lives for the better, through the support and encouragement of their peers," says Hefta-Gaub.

Sweat365.com is a business based on a compelling story, one that includes many of the same elements used to shape a great narrative. There's a *protagonist*, Sweat365.com, which is proposing a solution to change people's fitness habits.

There are *antagonists*, competitors in the fitness space. There are *vivid characters* such as Hefta-Gaub, who overcame his own struggle with obesity. There's *conflict*, the struggle of overweight Americans to become more active. And there's *resolution*, success in overcoming the conflict to lead a healthier life.

Like Sweat365.com, every company can tell the larger company story in a way that's compelling and attracts a high level of interest. It's not just about a non-descript company launching a new product or service. It's about vivid, real-life characters who must overcome obstacles to accomplish a goal that addresses an important customer need. Telling the overall story of your company brings your organization, your people, and your products to life. Not only does it mirror the way a good journalist reports a story, it's also a way to capture and hold the attention of the audiences you hope to reach, drawing them further into your story in the same way great novelists persuade their readers to keep turning the page.

"It's important to recognize that reporters are storytellers themselves and that their readers are best able to understand subjects as memorable, human stories as opposed to a list of facts and figures," says Caroline Boren, Alaska Airlines' managing director of corporate and strategic communications. "Anytime you plan to have a conversation with a reporter, it helps to consciously stop and ask yourself, 'What is the story?' and 'What is the most memorable or visual way I can tell it?'"

THE COMPELLING NATURE OF STORIES

Why does formulating an overarching story lead to greater exposure for your organization? Because a great story is inherently compelling. Stories arouse a listener's emotions, not just their intellect. They draw us into the drama, motivating us to learn about the dynamics of an organization. They are easy to remember. And they have the power to shift perceptions and accelerate change.

Stories have been an important part of our experience for as long as humans have walked the earth. "The use of the story not only to delight but to instruct and lead has long been a part of culture," writes Peter Guber, CEO of Mandalay Entertainment Group, in *Harvard Business Review*. "We can trace it back thousands of years to the days of the shaman around the tribal fire. It was he who recorded the oral history of the tribe, encoding its beliefs, values, and rules in the tales of its great heroes, of its triumphs and tragedies."[1]

Throughout human history, stories have been fundamental to the way we think and make sense of our world. The ability of stories to engage and create meaning has been confirmed through numerous studies and reports. For example, in his book *Literary Mind: The Origins of Thought and Language*, cognitive scientist, linguist, and author Mark Turner argues that the human mind is essentially literary. "Narrative imagining—story—is the fundamental instrument of thought," he writes. "Rational capacities depend on it. It is our chief means of looking into the future, of predicting, of planning, and of explaining. It is a literary capacity indispensable to human cognition generally."[2]

As they have in the past, stories continue to play a powerful role today, helping us bridge the gap between experience and communication. From early childhood onward, stories are all around us. They help us grasp ideas and shape our view of the world. When we were children, our parents read to us or shared their own stories. In school, we told our own stories during "show and tell" and listened to those of our classmates. As adults, stories continue to help us make sense of complex experiences. We share our stories with friends and family over dinner. We absorb stories through books, movies, plays, and other entertainment. We hear them while standing in the grocery line, watching the nightly news, and working at the office.

As business executives have come to recognize the power of storytelling, it has begun to make its way into organizations as a way to unite employees around a common goal. Says Stephen Denning, author of *The Springboard: How Storytelling Ignites Action in Knowledge-Era Organizations*, "Storytelling gets inside the minds of the individuals who collectively make up the organization and affects how they think, worry, wonder, agonize and dream about themselves and in the process create and re-create their organization. Storytelling enables the individuals in an organization to see themselves and the organization in a different light, and accordingly make decisions and change their behavior in accordance with these new perceptions, insights and identities."[3]

Stories are capable of turning soulless data into powerful drama that spurs people into action. Writes Guber, "Storytelling . . . is one of the world's most powerful tools for achieving astonishing results. For the leader, storytelling is action oriented—a force for turning dreams into goals and then into results."[4]

Henry Luce and Briton Hadden understood the power of storytelling and turned this knowledge into a lasting business success. The 1923 cofounders of *Time* magazine, Luce and Hadden transformed the world of journalism by taking the dry facts that dominated newspapers at the time and transforming them into vivid, persuasive news summaries. Their writing style proved to be so successful that it eventually gave rise to the formats used by several other weekly magazines such as *Newsweek, U.S. News & World Report*, and *People* magazines. Storytelling has since become a key component of news stories published by the *Wall Street Journal* and other daily newspapers around the world. Today it's become the central avenue through which journalists write and broadcast the news.

Gerry Spence on Discovering the Story

Storytelling is fundamental to the way trial lawyer Gerry Spence presents every case he takes on. Recognized nationwide for his powerful courtroom victories, Spence turns the injustices facing his clients into powerful courtroom melodramas that capture the hearts and minds of the jury. "Everything in life is a story. Everything," he writes in his book *Win Your Case*.[10]

Great lawyers are also great storytellers, according to Spence. "If we are to be successful in presenting our case we must not only discover its story, we must become good storytellers as well," he writes. "Every trial, every presentation, every plea for change, every argument for justice is a story."

So how does one become a great storyteller? By putting oneself inside the skin of the clients whose story we are telling, Spence writes. By feeling things the way they felt them and reliving the experience the way they did.

Although Spence is talking about storytelling as it relates to law, the same concepts can be applied to the business world. It's not just about a company that produced a new product. "Nothing happens to heat the blood when we read abstract language," Spence writes. Instead, you need to ask the questions that will bring the story to life. Ask the founder of your company to walk you through his experience in the present tense. What is he doing when the idea for the product first pops into his mind? What triggers the idea? Where is he, and what is he wearing? How does he feel when he first thinks of the idea? Is he excited? Does he feel it's a pipe dream? Whom does he first talk to about it? What is that person's reaction? What happens next?

Asking to be walked through the story enables us to really feel it, and by really feeling it, we can bring it to life to the audiences to which we want to communicate it. "The best way to tell the story is always from the inside out," Spence writes. "It's hard to tell our story until we know it—that is, until we've *felt it*—heard it with our third ear, seen it with the eyes of our client, until we have been gripped by it in deep places, and have finally lived it."

Spence recommends brainstorming with others to clarify the theme of the story and to figure out what questions you need to ask to make the story more vivid and memorable. He also recommends telling the story to friends, colleagues, and significant others to see which parts they personally relate to. Testing the story before communicating it to the media, a potential investor, or other target audiences helps ensure that we are telling it in a way that truly resonates.

"The stories that each of us have experienced, although with differing details, are the same in their substance," Spence writes. "For every story we hear we inhabit part of that story as our own."

THE KEY ELEMENTS OF A COMPELLING STORY

Telling the story of your company draws your audiences into your business in the same way a novel captivates a reader, creating a powerful way to shift perceptions. "I think that we human beings have always enjoyed great stories," says Lee Weinstein, principal of Lee Weinstein & Associates and the former director of global corporate communications for Nike. "It's part of who we are. It's built into our evolution. How you tell a story and where you tell a story are really important, and I think PR really allows us to do that in a powerful way."

So how do you go about crafting your company story? First, you need to have a clear idea of the value proposition of your company. "It all starts with the company's vision and mission," says Weinstein. "At Nike, our mission is to provide the innovation and inspiration to every athlete in the world. If you think about innovation and inspiration first, then everything that you do in PR should be innovative and inspirational, from the writing to the images to the selection of the campaigns you're going to really get behind."

In addition, your overarching story should have all the elements of a great narrative: a protagonist, an antagonist, a lively cast of characters, a setting, a plot, a conflict, and a resolution:

The Protagonist

The protagonist is always your company and the products and services you're trying to sell. In the case of Sweat365.com, for example, the protagonist is the company itself, along with its goal of drawing people to its social networking site.

The Antagonist

The antagonist is usually your company's major competitors. The antagonists for Sweat365.com are competitors in the fitness space, such as Active.com or Runner's World. Other antagonists can include the broader social network sites such as Facebook and MySpace.

The Cast of Characters

Every great narrative should include a vivid cast of characters who bring your company story to life and will probably include your CEO and a small group of company executives. Who are the interesting, charismatic individuals who can best tell the various pieces of your story? For Sweat365.com, Brad Hefta-Gaub is the most compelling character to tell the business side of the story while cofounder and CTO Phil Sabin is the best person to tell the technology piece of the story. The cast of characters for Sweat365.com also includes users of the site whose lives have been changed by the site. Engaging a vivid cast of characters automatically makes your story more compelling by adding the essential element of human interest.

The Setting

The setting is where the dynamics of your industry category come into play. What is the competitive landscape? What pressures are your company facing in the broader marketplace? Do statistics or background information help reinforce your story? For Sweat365.com, the setting is the overall problem of obesity in America, bolstered by the statistics that more than one-third of U.S. adults are considered obese and two-thirds are considered overweight.[5] It's also the competitive landscape and the fact that while social networks are taking off, few to date have been created that target audiences with the same specific interest.

The Plot

In fiction, the plot is the action of the story or a series of incidents that take place over time. With your company story, it's the series of milestones your company is hoping to reach. Writes Guber, "Listeners must remain curious and in suspense—wondering what's going to happen to them next—while trusting that it is safe to give themselves over to the journey and that the destination will be worthwhile."[6]

You can foreshadow the plot by telling journalists the milestones you expect to reach over a specific time period and then release each significant milestone as a separate announcement as the plot unfolds. When Sweat365.com was launched, for example, executives let the media know they would hear back from the company when it secured additional funding. By doing that, they were teeing up the next story and foreshadowing the action to come.

The Conflict

The conflict is a series of challenges you need to overcome, a consumer mindset you need to change, or a competitor you need to beat out for your company to be successful. In his book, *News Reporting and Writing*, Columbia University Professor Emeritus Melvin Mencher writes, "Strife, antagonism, and confrontation have been the building blocks of stories since people drew pictures of the hunt on the walls of their caves. Man's struggles with himself and his gods, a Hamlet or a Prometheus, are the essentials of drama."[7]

For Sweat365.com, the conflict is overcoming the lack of motivation that prevents Americans from living a healthy lifestyle. On a more personal level, it's the struggle with oneself to stay in shape. The more clearly you can describe the obstacles your company needs to overcome to attain success, the more compelling your story will be.

Resolution

The resolution is the story's ending. Did your company reach its goals? Did it accomplish the milestones it set out to achieve? For Sweat365.com, success means becoming a well-known social networking site that plays a central role in overcoming obesity. It also means truly helping people get in shape. While in reality, the plot continues to unfold as long as your company is in business, you can view the resolution as what happens over a specific time frame, such as what your company accomplished by year end or during the period covered by the PR plan.

Anne Lamott and the Importance of Drama

Whether or not we admit it, we're all drawn to drama. Whether it's a great novel, a news article, or hearsay about someone we know, drama is at the heart of any great story. It's what holds people's attention.

In her book *Bird by Bird: Some Instructions on Writing and Life*, Anne Lamott says the basic formula for drama is *setup, buildup,* and *payoff*—just as in a joke: "The setup tells us what the game is. The buildup is where you put in all the moves, the forward motion, where you get all the meat off the turkey. The payoff answers the question, Why are we here anyway? What is it that you've been trying to give?"[11]

While crafting your pitch, pay close attention to where the drama lies and bring it to the forefront for your audience. What is the *setup*? What does the competitive landscape look like? What challenges does your industry face? What problems do your customers experience? This will set the stage for your announcement.

Second, what is the *buildup*? What obstacles did your staff overcome to develop a new product or service? What other obstacles did your organization encounter to get to this point? Telling a great story always involves forward movement.

Finally, what is the *payoff*? Are you releasing a breakthrough product that will change the industry? Are you solving a difficult problem for customers? In what way are you changing people's lives? Your story must discuss the significance of your announcement and how it will change the situation you discussed in the setup.

Pulling out the drama captures people's interest and makes your story far more memorable. As Anne Lamott writes, "Drama must move forward and upward, or the seats on which the audience is sitting will become very hard and uncomfortable . . . There must be movement."

APPLYING THE OTHER RULES OF NARRATIVE

In addition to the key elements described above, other rules apply when developing a great narrative, many of which also hold true as you craft your company story:

Show, Don't Tell

It's often said that when writing a play or novel, you should show, don't tell. If you're describing a character, for example, it has less impact to tell readers, "She felt sad," than to show readers what you observe: "Tears came to her eyes, and her voice quivered." In the same way, you don't want to simply make the claim that your company "successfully" launched its new product. Instead you need to show journalists that your launch was successful by backing up the claim with specific details: the fact that 3,000 consumers attended the launch, for example and that your company sold 1,000 widgets during the first week, greatly exceeding expectations.

Be Selective

The art of omission is key to producing a great work of art, whether it be a novel, a piece of music, or a painting. Similarly, your company's story should always be simple and succinct. Don't get bogged down in relaying every detail about your company, your product, or a particular event. What is the one thing you want your audiences to remember? What are the three most compelling facts that back up the point you're making? Select only the essential information, and leave the rest out.

Make It Interesting

For a novel to be compelling, the story must be unique, unusual, or unexpected. In the same way, your overarching story and each individual announcement should be interesting and newsworthy. Mencher, the Columbia University professor, attributes the newsworthiness of an idea or event to one or more of the following seven factors:

- Impact: events that are likely to affect many people
- Timeliness: events that are immediate, recent
- Prominence: events involving well-known people or institutions
- Proximity: events in the circulation or broadcast area (of the media outlet running the story)
- Conflict: events that reflect clashes between people or institutions
- The bizarre: events that deviate sharply from the expected experiences of everyday life
- Currency: events and situations that are being talked about

What makes your story unique, and why should journalists care? You can use these seven factors to test whether your story will be of interest to the media outlets you target.

Use Analogies

Analogies provide a great way to tell a story in a memorable way. Over the years, authors have written successful business books drawing upon colorful analogies in the worlds of war, sports, martial arts, fishing, science, and theater, among other topics. For example, in their book *Judo Strategy*, coauthors David B. Yoffie and Mary Kwak examine the strategic mindset of judo masters, turning this thinking into lessons for business executives. "Metaphors can be great motivational tools because they are usually easy to understand and hard to forget," Yoffie writes.[8]

Leverage Classic Story Themes

Another way to tell a compelling story is to frame yours using myths and other classical story themes such as those of Pegasus, Midas, Ulysses, Hamlet, King Lear, Creon and his fatal flaw of hubris, the philosopher's stone, or the hare and the tortoise. Classic stories like these provide a conceptual framework you can use to tell your story with greater impact. Gerry Spence, the criminal defense lawyer, knows this. For him, it's not a case of Karen Silkwood versus Kerr-McGee. It's David versus Goliath. Kerr-McGee is "the men in grey suits," and "the little guy" is Karen Silkwood. Spence frames every case around a conceptual structure that allows jurors to view the situation in the way he intends. And with that, he's able to defeat billion-dollar multinational corporations such as Kerr-McGee.

"Classical themes continue to pervade all forms of media, including news reporting," says Caroline Boren of Alaska Airlines. "Capitalizing on the human appeal of these oft-repeated themes is another method for helping the reporter write a compelling story and maximizing your PR opportunities."

BENEFITS OF A COMPELLING STORY

Crafting an overall company story serves many critical purposes. First, it enables your company to make sure every individual news announcement ties into the broader story you want to tell. Second, it provides a framework for deciding which stories to pursue. It also enables you to tell your story with greater conviction, create a compelling pitch, and tailor it to fit the specific audiences you seek to reach.

Describing the Forest, Not Just the Trees

Companies tend to focus on isolated news announcements without understanding that each individual announcement accrues to the larger company story they want to tell. If an individual announcement doesn't feed into the larger story, you run the risk of confusing your audiences. They may think you're telling a story other than the one you intend. Or they may perceive your news as random or insignificant.

Conversely, when each announcement contributes to your overall company story, your PR efforts become focused and meaningful. In the same way that a novel's subplot must relate to the overall plot, each announcement your company makes will have the biggest impact if it closely relates to the overarching story. We often remind our clients to explain the forest, not just the tree. If you're simply focused on each individual announcement, you're only telling the journalist about the tree. If you want journalists to understand the significance of your news, you must also explain the ways that each tree fits into the larger picture of the forest as a whole.

For example, if Sweat365.com simply issues a press release announcing it received $900,000 from two venture capitalists, the reaction from a journalist might be, "Why should I care?" But if Sweat365.com ties this announcement back to its overarching story—that the company wants consumers to embrace a social networking platform that helps them become fit—suddenly the news becomes more exciting. A better way to frame the story is to say that venture capitalists see great promise in the Sweat365.com business model. The evidence? The willingness of two venture capitalists to contribute $900,000 in the first round of funding.

Providing a Focused Framework

Not only does linking each news announcement back to the overarching story enable you to attract the widest exposure for each announcement, it also helps you decide which news announcements should be pursued and which should be discarded as tangential or irrelevant. For example, many of our clients are requested by partners to issue joint press releases. Having an overarching story helps them determine whether each of these opportunities ties back to the story they wish to tell. Knowing this, they can more easily decide if they should invest the resources to promote the announcement to the media, let their partner carry the weight, or refrain from participating in the announcement altogether.

Telling Your Story with Conviction

Tying each announcement to the broader story of your company imbues the news with greater meaning. It's simply more memorable, which makes it more likely people will pass it on to others. It also makes it easier to get behind the story and pitch it with greater conviction. For example, tying news announcements about Sweat365.com back to the larger story allowed executives to get really passionate about their story pitches. The announcement wasn't just about another venture capitalist investing in the company. It was about obtaining the funding that was critical to help adults in our society lose weight, a cause people are passionate about. Knowing your overarching story makes it clear why you're pitching an announcement. And if you're able to participate emotionally, that passion will be contagious.

Tailoring Your Story to Your Target Audience

While an overarching story is important, by itself it's not enough. For your story to be compelling, it must be relevant to the audience you're targeting. A middle-aged woman is not likely to pick up a novel aimed at teenage boys. Nor is she likely to read an article about men's razor blades. Writes Peter Guber, "The great storyteller takes time to understand what his listeners know about, care about, and want to hear. Then he crafts the essential elements of the story so that they elegantly resonate with those needs, starting where the listeners are and bringing them along on a satisfying emotional journey."[9]

In the same way, you need to find a compelling news hook that matches the interests of each media outlet you're targeting. When Hefta-Gaub tells the story of Sweat365.com, the angle he emphasizes entirely depends on the audience he's trying to reach. "During our launch, we worked entirely with business press, so I talked about the business aspects of our strategy—the fact that fitness is a growing market and that we were taking an entirely unique approach," he says. "If I was talking to a lifestyle reporter, I might tell the story from more of a human interest perspective, perhaps about the thirty-year-old woman from Virginia who didn't think she could even run a mile and ended up running a half-marathon because she wanted to blog about how she finished the whole thing without stopping." (Please see Principle 3 for more information about targeting your audiences.)

Note that each of the stories Hefta-Gaub tells relates closely back to the overarching story of the company. It simply does so in a way that matches the interests of the media outlet he wants to reach.

Once you've crafted your overarching story and developed a series of targeted pitches that match the interests of the media outlet you want to reach, you've completed the first step of developing a great relationship with the media by making sure every story pitch is relevant and compelling. In Principle 7, we'll set you on the path to successful story placement by discussing the key steps required to forge lasting relationships with the media.

BUILD MEDIA RELATIONSHIPS FOR STRATEGIC ADVANTAGE

At its core, public relations is about building and maintaining positive relationships, and there's no place more critical than the media arena. A strategic approach to PR requires forging meaningful ongoing relationships with the reporters with whom you work. Accomplishing that entails choosing the best spokespeople within your organization, knowing how to give a great interview, and adding value in a myriad of other ways that result in mutually beneficial relationships for the media and your company.

CHOOSING YOUR SPOKESPEOPLE

As with any interpersonal relationship, developing a good one with the media requires sincerity, accountability, and awareness of the other's needs. The place to start is to choose the right spokespeople for your company. How many individuals you select as spokespeople depends on the size of the company and the complexity of the information to be conveyed. In a small company, you may want your CEO to talk about the business direction, your CFO to discuss funding, and your CTO to explain the innovative technology you just developed and patented. In a larger company, you'll want to offer different spokespeople to serve as experts on the various products and services you offer. There's no rule about the number of spokespeople you have. What's important, however, is that all spokespeople are properly trained to understand the workings of the media and stay up-to-date on your organization's messaging.

In most cases, you'll want one or more company executives to serve as spokespeople rather than assigning the role to a PR person. Reporters usually want to talk to the lead expert on the issue because they're the ones most familiar with the topic and can talk about it firsthand. They get frustrated when the PR specialist acts as the intermediary and isn't able to answer questions in a detailed manner. Here are eight questions to consider when choosing the best ambassadors to speak for your company:

- *Are they great communicators?* A great spokesperson understands your company's messages, can clearly articulate them, and can stay on message. Writes former presidential media adviser Robert Ailes in his book, *You Are the Message*, "Remember back to a moment when you know you were communicating effectively because you absolutely believed in what you were saying. Remember how you felt? Harness that power and you will be successful at communications."[1]

- *Are they passionate and enthusiastic about your organization's work?* A great spokesperson also realizes the way he acts exemplifies the message. "When you communicate with someone, it's not just the words you choose to send to the other person that make up the message," writes Ailes. "You're also sending signals about what kind of person *you* are—by your eyes, your facial expression, your body movement, your vocal pitch, tone, volume, and intensity, your commitment to your message, your sense of humor, and many other factors."[2] If you're committed to your message, if you can demonstrate energy and enthusiasm, it will be infectious and lead to better results.

- *Are they likeable?* In addition, a great spokesperson has excellent interpersonal skills. Often a technologist or engineer may step into the spokesperson role, but if he doesn't have strong interpersonal skills, it can present a challenge. It's best to choose someone who's gregarious and outgoing, who has a sense of humor, and who can work to meet the needs of the reporter with whom he's talking.

- *Do they have good listening skills?* Being a great spokesperson also involves listening intently to the reporter's question and then trying to answer it. Therefore, it's critical to choose someone who's a good listener in addition to a good talker.

- *Are they insightful enough to understand what's beyond the question?* Sometimes busy reporters walk into an interview without a detailed understanding of the topic they're planning to write about and so may not know the right questions to ask. A great spokesperson has the ability to say, "Oh, so what you're really trying to understand is X, Y, or Z." She has the capacity to understand what the reporter's underlying objective is when he asks a question and then make sure it's addressed.

- *Are they patient and willing to educate?* Some people get frustrated with reporters when they don't understand their business. They're not aware that reporters are required to write about a broad range of topics. If you're short or disrespectful, it can harm the long-term relationship. Conversely, exhibiting patience and being willing to educate forges a trusting, ongoing relationship.

- *Do they value the media and the role it plays?* Some executives don't understand the powerful role that journalists can have on the shape of their company and its products. As a consequence, they think that talking to the media isn't a valuable use of their time. A great spokesperson understands why talking to the media is important to their business and will commit the time needed to do a great job.

- *Are they comfortable and prepared?* Executives often fear the media. They're worried about saying something that will embarrass them or their company, or they fear they'll be misquoted. "In my experience with media training sessions, people are terrified of reporters," says media, business, and executive coach Elaine Long. "They're really focused on themselves, and not saying something that will make them sound stupid or that they'll get in trouble for. They don't understand that reporters aren't out to get them. They're just like anybody who has a job to do." Great spokespeople are comfortable speaking to reporters and talk openly. They also approach encounters with the media well-prepared and walk into the interview knowing what the reporter wants to write about as well as the messages they want to convey.

Developing a Great Relationship with Reporters

Want to develop a great relationship with the media? Here's some advice from business executives and PR practitioners from a wide range of organizations:

"I always try to approach a media story from the angle of what a reporter would be interested in versus what it is we want to get across. Find out what they're interested in first, and then figure out how your story plays into that. Also, try to separate yourself and not make it personal or emotional in any way. They've got a job to do, and they're just trying to do it. The more you can understand that, the more you can maintain a positive working relationship."

—**Brad Stevens**, former vice president of U.S. marketing, Starbucks

"Number one, don't waste their time with something that isn't newsworthy. Number two, when you have something newsworthy, make sure you're taking it to the right media outlet. You'd better know who you're going to, what that person has written about, and what their audience is interested in. When you really know your media outlets and your reporters, you can say, 'Yes, this story would work for them; I think they would find interest in it,' and then you go to them."

—**Keith Lindenburg**, director, national public relations, Deloitte Services LP

"Relationships require trust, they're two-way, and they're mutually beneficial. They take time, and they take track records. When I was at Nike, we really tried to value those relationships. We had a rule that everybody had to be available 24/7 by phone, we beefed up our Web site to make it easier for the media to reach us, and we had a policy of returning calls the day they were received. We also tried to get to the media and check in with them so they weren't always coming to us."

—**Lee Weinstein**, former director of global corporate communications, Nike

"You want to be fair to all of the media outlets. Not having a bias is pretty important. I try to have a lot of expertise in the area I'm working in and provide more information in the interview than what we included in the press release so they feel they're getting more information by talking to us. The other thing that's important is making myself available to comment on the things that are going on in the market, being willing to be a source they can go to. Finally, I often thank them for writing such a good article so that I continue to build the relationship. All of these things are pretty important."

—**Steve Brodie**, chief products and marketing officer, Skytap

"My personal opinion is that you need to be respectful of reporters and their time. That's pretty obvious, but I think a lot of people try to get the media on the phone just because they want to talk. You're wasting their time if you're doing that. You should set up calls only if you have something to talk about, something that would be truly valuable to the media. It really has to be a mutually beneficial relationship. It can't be all about the company."

—**Andrea Mocherman**, manager of marketing communications,
SNAPin Software

"I think it's important to take a long-term perspective and to recognize that your relationship with the media is a game of averages, and you're not always going to bat 1,000. Ultimately, approaching the relationship from the perspective of your long-term batting average is going to be more important than one-off damage control. Maybe I can win on this story, but if it's going to harm my long-term credibility with that reporter, it's just not worth it. Ask yourself if there's something you can do today to nurture the long-term perception of yourself and your organization. And if there is, that's more important than short-term gain."

—**Caroline Boren**, managing director of corporate
and strategic communications, Alaska Airlines

PREPARING FOR THE INTERVIEW

A successful media interview is all about preparation. When spokespeople take the interview seriously and make the time to prepare, they tend to do a great job. It's only when they think, "I've done this a million times. I can wing it" that the trouble happens.

If you're new to media relations, consider taking a media training class or ask your PR specialist to coach you. It's one thing to read about the right techniques and another thing entirely to practice them. When we provide media training sessions, we offer executives the opportunity to be videotaped, which can be a very powerful educational tool.

To prepare for the interview, you'll want to gather background information about the reporter and the publication. What is the focus of the publication? What beat does the reporter cover? What other stories has she written about your category, and what slant did she take? How knowledgeable is she about your business? If you're a company executive, ask your PR specialist to gather this information. If you're the PR specialist, proactively gather this information and provide it to the company spokesperson to help him prepare for the call.

You also need to gather some specifics about what the story is about and how it arose. Is the reporter contacting you because she's working on a feature for the summer issue? Does she want your organization's perspective on a news event? How is she planning to frame the story, and who else is she planning to interview?

A savvy PR specialist will also obtain a list of questions in advance. One way to go about this is to say, "You know, I want to make sure we're well prepared and are using your time wisely. Would it be possible to share some of your questions with me in advance of the call? That way I can make sure that Joe Smith is ready to answer them." Be aware that some reporters will refuse to do this while others will always say yes. Even if the reporter doesn't stick to the questions she sends you, it's still helpful because it provides insight into the reporter's general direction.

You may also want to suggest some questions the reporter should ask. One way to approach this is to say, "We think your readers may be interested in issue X. These are some of the questions you might want to ask to get insight into this issue." Many reporters cover a broad range of topics and don't have a deep level of insight into the specific issues facing your company. They will often appreciate the extra insight you can provide because it can result in a better story.

In addition to obtaining questions from the reporter, you'll want to anticipate the hard questions. You can expect reporters' questions to vary according to where your company is in its life cycle. If you work for a start-up company, for example, reporters are likely to ask about the benefits of your product or service, the viability of your business model, and how you differ from the competition. If you're a category leader, you may get some tough questions about antitrust issues or your plans for meeting the next round of revenue goals. On the other hand, it's doubtful you'll get questions about the viability of your business model since it's already been proven to work over time.

After you've drafted a set of questions that you anticipate being asked, prepare some solid answers. Memorize the messages you're planning to communicate and practice delivering them. Prepare statistics and solid examples to back up any claims and bring your messages to life. Keep in mind that reporters always love a great quote, and develop short sound bites that they'll be tempted to use. We had a client who was a master at this. He'd always think through the messages he wanted to convey in advance, and he'd challenge us as his PR team to come up with punchy sound bites that illustrated the point. They were always clever; some were double entendres. Our client incorporated these sound bites into his interviews and was quoted widely.

MANAGING THE INTERVIEW PROCESS

Reporters often get on the phone with a company spokesperson only to find that he's not prepared, can't talk about the topic in an understandable way, or is the wrong person to speak to entirely. This can be a frustrating experience for the reporter and the spokesperson. A knowledgeable spokesperson who can tell a captivating story goes a long way in the development of a great rapport with reporters. Here are eleven best practices you can develop to help ensure successful interviews:

1. *Get the interview off to the right start.* When you get on the phone with a reporter, don't use your mobile phone, multitask, or allow yourself to be distracted. Separate yourself from what you had been doing and give the reporter your full attention. To make sure you and the reporter are on the same page, you'll want to establish several ground rules right at the beginning of the interview. First, restate the purpose of the call so you have a clear understanding of the story the reporter wants to write. Second, ask the reporter how much time she has for the call so you can plan a reasonable level of detail for your answers. With many media interviews, we've gotten into the practice of recording the conversation and then developing a transcript to give to the reporter and the spokesperson. This helps the reporter accurately quote your company spokesperson. It's also helpful for the spokesperson because it allows him to review his messages verbatim and train other spokespeople within the company. If you want to record the conversation, make sure you obtain the reporter's agreement at the beginning of the call.

2. *Include your PR specialist in the interview.* Company executives don't often think it is necessary to invite their PR person to join the interview, yet failing to do so is a missed opportunity. PR representatives provide a second set of ears during the conversation. Because their job is to listen to make sure the executive is delivering the right messages in a way the reporter understands, they can provide feedback after the call. They can also step in during the call to add a point that hasn't been made, frame the information in a way that's positive, or check in with the reporter to make sure she's grasping the information the executive is trying to convey.

3. *Captivate interest.* You've prepared for the interview. Now's your chance to convey the information in a way that's going to resonate with readers. Stay on message and be succinct. Use the sound bites you've developed. Make your story easy to understand, and tell it with enthusiasm. Back up your claims with substantive examples and proof points. Don't just say your software is the best—tell the reporter that it won fourteen awards during the past six months and that four out of five customers interviewed by a third-party analyst firm rated it the best. You need to have the substance to back up your claims; otherwise, the reporter's going to get frustrated.

4. *Check in with the reporter.* It's amazing how often spokespeople think they have clearly answered a reporter's question when it turns out the reporter is either looking for an answer to another question or hasn't completely understood the spokesperson's point. At some point during the interview, the executive or PR person should check in with the reporter to clarify her thought process and make sure her questions are being answered. We often say, "Hey, Jane, we've covered a lot of information thus far. Are we addressing the questions you had in mind? Is any of this unclear? What do you think about all of this?" If you don't check in during the conversation, you may get off the phone thinking the reporter completely understood what you were talking about, only to read a story that completely misses the mark.

5. *Keep the conversation on track.* Reporters typically don't have a lot of time to spare. Most work on tight deadlines and have little time to report and write their stories. Be cognizant of their time by staying on message and getting to the point quickly. State your most important information upfront, and then back it up with solid facts and examples. Say as much as is necessary to thoroughly make your point, then stop talking and wait for the next question.

6. *Answer questions directly.* If you watch the Sunday talk shows, you'll often observe politicians trying to duck uncomfortable questions posed by reporters. This practice irritates reporters and quickly erodes the relationship. If a reporter asks a question you can't or don't want to answer, never evade the question or say, "No comment." Instead acknowledge the question, and tell the reporter why you can't answer it. For example, "We're not prepared to talk about that right now because we've signed a non-disclosure agreement with a customer" or whatever the case may be. Similarly, if the reporter has told you in advance that the conversation will focus on one topic but starts probing about a more controversial subject that your organization doesn't want to address, the PR representative should step in and say, "You know, Jane, when I agreed to put you in touch with Joe, my understanding was that you were going to focus on X, Y, and Z. We're really not prepared to talk about Q because we have to respect employee privacy issues, but what I can tell you is . . ."

7. *Use bridging techniques to convey your message.* A great spokesperson knows how to use bridging techniques as a way of making the transition from the question being asked to the message he wants to convey. For example, you might say, "Jane, that's a really good question. Let me give you a little background." You then give the reporter the

background you want to convey leading up to answering the question. Other examples of bridging techniques might be, "That speaks to a bigger point, which is . . . ," "The real issue here is . . . ," and "What's important to remember, however, is . . ."

8. *Be careful about "off the record."* Providing information to reporters off the record can be a great way to forge a stronger relationship. However, extreme caution is a must here. This is definitely terrain for the experienced spokesperson and not the novice. If you do decide to take this route, make sure you're talking to a reporter you trust. Make sure you clarify what "off the record" means before you agree to divulge any information. Technically, "off the record" means the reporter may not publish the information at all whereas "not for attribution" means the reporter can use the information but must keep your identity anonymous. If you decide to allow the reporter to publish the information without referring to you by name, you'll need to negotiate exactly how you'll be characterized in the story. In the context of what's being said, a quote attributed to "the CEO of a small Seattle-based mobile wireless company" may turn out not to be anonymous at all.

9. *Don't be defensive or dismissive.* If a reporter asks a tough question, it's important never to become defensive or dismissive. If you think the question is irrelevant or unimportant, take a deep breath and a step back and then politely answer it anyway. If you're defensive or dismissive, you're likely going to end up hurting the reporter's feelings and harming the relationship. Be friendly, patient, and polite, and work with the reporter to get your story told accurately.

10. *Listen for clues.* During the interview, listen for clues about the reporter's approach to the story. This will enable you to think through ways to bolster your organization's position with additional information or interviews after the call. If the reporter bombards you with tough questions, you'll know she may write a negative article. If this happens, the spokesperson and PR person may want to brainstorm about whom else they can put the reporter in touch with to shape her perspective. Perhaps the perspective of a customer, a partner, or an industry analyst may bolster your argument. If you do suggest another interview, however, make sure the person truly has something significant to add that hasn't already been discussed. Otherwise, the reporter will feel that you're wasting her time, and your organization will lose credibility.

11. *Review your performance.* It's important to debrief once the interview is over to learn what went well and what could have gone better. If you're the company executive, ask your PR specialist for feedback and take it to heart. Read the transcript to review the messages you conveyed and how you delivered them. If you're the PR specialist, and the reporter has requested follow-up information, use the opportunity to ask for feedback on how she thinks the call went. Taking the time to debrief helps ensure that you're meeting the reporter's needs and are improving your media interview skills over time.

Handling a High Volume of Media Interest

Many organizations have to work proactively to attract media interest. But for some companies, the challenge is to respond effectively to a high volume of media requests. Perhaps your organization has broad recognition, and media interest is consistently high. Or perhaps you've just issued a popular announcement or are immersed in a crisis and are receiving a large volume of media inquiries over a limited period of time.

"One of the things that's different about Second Life is the sheer volume of interest," says Catherine Smith, director of marketing and brand strategy for Linden Lab, creator of Second Life. "I've never experienced anything like it before. At first, I didn't do any proactive PR because I was completely immersed in responding to requests for information."

So what do you do when you're getting a large volume of media inquiries? Here are five tips to help you react in the best way possible:

1. *Set up a response system.* Designate one person or more to handle the incoming requests, and make it clear to everyone in the organization who's authorized to respond and what to do if the media contacts them. Develop relationships with experts in your organization; help them understand your need for them to respond quickly as requests for information come in.

2. *Track your calls.* Make sure you track all media requests your organization receives. Keep a spreadsheet that lists who called, the date of the inquiry, the media outlet, what the inquiry was, who handled the request, and when it was responded to. This will help you analyze the types of inquiries you're getting and when you're receiving them.

3. *Develop talking points.* Create talking points to help your company respond quickly to multiple requests for the same information. Develop a list of experts in the organization whom you can contact for specific information.

4. *Respond promptly to all requests.* If a reporter calls or sends an e-mail, make a point to return his or her call within the hour. Work to understand the reporter's questions and the story the reporter plans to write. Make sure you know the reporter's deadline, and provide him with information in a timely manner. Be sure to ask the reporter when the story will appear.

5. *Focus your efforts.* When you're receiving a high volume of calls, it's impossible to grant every reporter an interview with the CEO or your organization's top executives. Learn the target audience of each media outlet, consider the story the reporter is writing, decide whether the opportunity fits with your company's business objectives, and be strategic about which interviews you set up. "Starbucks gets

a ton of press coverage, more than any other brand I've ever worked with," says Brad Stevens, Starbucks' former vice president of U.S. marketing. "When you're facing this situation, the question you need to ask yourself is, 'Are you being strategic around the kind of media you're generating? How much of your publicity is done to you versus you deciding how you want to influence it?'"

FORGING LASTING RELATIONSHIPS

Not only does forging great media relationships require giving great interviews, it entails maintaining the connection over time. Says Lee Weinstein, principal of Lee Weinstein & Associates and Nike's former director of global corporation communications, "My underlying philosophy about public relations is that relationships are absolutely key. I mean, the title of our profession has 'relations' in it. And all great relationships are both mutually beneficial and have an element of trust." Here are some additional strategies you can implement to build and maintain meaningful relationships:

1. *Make yourself available.* If you're distributing a press release or your company is making a story pitch to the media, it's imperative that the spokesperson be available to talk to reporters. That may seem obvious, but we've actually seen companies fail to plan for this. For example, one company we worked with actually organized a press tour for a specific week without first confirming the dates with the spokesperson. It turned out that the spokesperson had scheduled an eye surgery right before the tour, had no time to prepare, and had to wear dark sunglasses because his eyes were swollen, which made a strange impression with the media. If you're releasing news, you need to make sure you're available to respond to the media's calls, know what messages you want to convey, and understand the overall objectives of your effort.

2. *Be aware of deadlines.* Along the same lines, it's important to respond quickly to information requests from the media. When a reporter calls, we make a point to call her back within the same hour. Once you know the information she's seeking, it's OK to allow yourself some time to collect your thoughts and any additional information you need to participate in the interview. However, always ask the reporter what her deadline is and agree on a specific time to call her back so you're sure to make her deadline.

3. *Suggest relevant story ideas.* A great way to develop lasting relationships with reporters is to develop a deep understanding of the specific beats

they cover and suggest relevant story ideas. As discussed in Principle 3, it's important to do your homework before calling a reporter to see what kinds of stories the publication writes about and what specific beat the reporter covers. There's nothing more frustrating to a busy reporter than to receive story pitches that are self-promotional, irrelevant, or off the mark. Conversely, there's nothing more helpful than to get a relevant, timely story idea. "I think it's important not to waste anyone's time but only bring reporters stories they're truly interested in," says Catherine Smith, director of marketing and brand strategy for Linden Lab. "Reporters get spammed with hundreds of press releases that aren't relevant to them. If you do that, I can guarantee they won't talk to you."

4. *Communicate frequently.* Even if you don't have a story idea that involves your company, you can keep your company top of mind with reporters by staying in touch with them regularly. If you do contact them, however, make sure you have something to offer that truly adds value. You may want to call them to share a piece of information about the industry that may help them do a better job or give them a quick call to bring them up-to-date about your company. "Rather than flooding reporters with the latest news, we spend a lot of time making informal phone calls," says Stan Sorensen, vice president of marketing at Egencia, an Expedia, Inc. company. "The reason why that's so important to us is that these folks are always working on stories, and our ultimate goal is to make sure our messages are included in any stories they're working on."

5. *Read what they write.* Another way to build relationships is to periodically read what reporters write and send an e-mail sharing your feedback on a story they wrote. Sending an occasional comment on a story they wrote shows you're paying attention and are interested in the work they do. Says Elaine Long, the media, business, and executive coach, "Building relationships requires learning about what the journalist is writing about and what their point of view is on things. People feel special when others take the opportunity to see and hear them."

6. *Get to know them personally.* As with any business relationship, it's a great idea to get to know the reporters you work with as human beings. When you're in town, ask them to lunch so you can get to know each other. Or get better acquainted on the phone. Perhaps the reporter just had a baby. Maybe she shares the same interest in running that you do. Perhaps she just published a book, and you decide to read it so that you can discuss it with her. When you get to know reporters on a personal level, all of a sudden they will welcome your phone calls. It also makes your job a lot more interesting and fun.

What to Do When the Story Is Inaccurate

You've completed the interview believing the reporter understood the topic and the messages you were trying to convey. But when you pick up the publication a few days later, you see that you've been misquoted or that the story contains inaccurate statements. What do you do?

If the mistake is insignificant, you may want to let it pass. Correcting a minor inaccuracy that doesn't affect the overall story probably isn't worth your energy. However, if the inaccuracy is important, you'll need to engage the reporter to find out what happened.

We recommend doing this in a deferential way that allows the reporter to save face. The reporter believes the story is accurate, so pointing out an inaccuracy will likely create cognitive dissonance. In this uncomfortable situation, it's important to be diplomatic and appeal to the reporter's desire to do a good job. For example, you might say, "I'm sure you're committed to writing accurate articles, and we must not have done a good job relaying our messages during the interview. I realize we were talking kind of fast, and perhaps we could have provided you with more detail on X, Y, and Z. Help us understand your perspective regarding what happened and what we can do differently to make sure future articles about our company are accurate."

When you've reached agreement with the reporter about the reason for the inaccuracy, request a correction. Then figure out the steps you can take to help the reporter write more accurate stories in the future. Perhaps you'll want to provide the reporter with a transcript of the call. Or maybe you'll want to circle back with the reporter after the next call to make sure he understood the discussion and determine whether he needs additional questions answered.

Along the same lines, if you believe the reporter to be hostile toward your organization or is covering your news in a biased manner, rather than cutting off the relationship, continue to work with him and strive to develop a better relationship over time. Refusing to work with a reporter doesn't accomplish anything. In most cases, the reporter will continue to cover your company without access to your side of the story, which only makes things worse. Perhaps you don't want to disclose everything about your company, but if you make the reporter feel slighted, it will only fuel the fire. In our minds, it's far better to continue to share your story and work to build a trusted relationship over time.

EMBARGOES AND EXCLUSIVES

Before you get on the phone with reporters, it's critical that you develop a strategy for releasing the news. With some announcements, organizations negotiate embargoes with reporters, requiring them to hold the news until a specific date and time. Companies also occasionally release the news to a single reporter as an exclusive. Before acting on either of those options, it's important to determine whether an embargo or an exclusive makes strategic sense.

Releasing News under Embargo

Occasionally an organization will release a news announcement under embargo—two or three weeks before planning to release it to the wire. Sharing your announcement with reporters far in advance helps them report the news accurately and thoroughly by giving them more time to research and write complex stories. It also offers you insight into the level of media interest in your announcement, allowing you to sweeten the news if interest is low. After speaking to reporters, for example, you may need to go back to the CEO and say, "We have spoken with five reporters, and none of them finds our news particularly significant. I think we could attract more coverage if we could provide five customers who can talk about the significance of our technology or if we could better articulate how our technology is leading the entire category in a new direction."

If you do release news under embargo, make sure the media outlet agrees to honor the embargo before you actually share the news. Never send reporters a press release that simply says, "Embargoed until January 1 at 10 a.m." unless you've first talked to them and secured their spoken or written agreement. Our experience is that most reporters will agree to an embargo if it is negotiated in advance. When you're embargoing a story, it's important to specify the exact hour the embargo is being lifted in addition to the day. If you simply say August 23, you can expect the news to hit at various times throughout the day, which might leave some media outlets with the perception that they were scooped.

Releasing News as an Exclusive

Another way to influence the coverage is to offer up the news as an exclusive to a single media outlet, allowing it alone to break the story. One scenario in which you might want to do this is if you work for a large company and the CEO's time is limited. For example, perhaps you know the story will have greater impact if Bill Gates grants an interview, but he has time for only one meeting, not fifteen. Alternatively, perhaps your organization has a limited budget and can't afford to go out on press tour. Giving the story to a single trusted reporter and allowing him to report it in detail may help you reap the strongest benefit with the resources you have.

Another situation in which an exclusive may make the most sense is if the story is complex and the significance will emerge only if the reporter provides a great deal of background analysis. Perhaps you're releasing news about a partnership deal, and the significance isn't immediately obvious. By providing a detailed briefing to one reporter who can bring the story to life, other reporters will often follow suit, reporting the full significance of the news based on the first story that appeared.

If you take this approach, we recommend you first weigh the impact an exclusive will have on your relationship with other media outlets. If you work for a start-up that's proactively seeking coverage, giving an exclusive to one publication may damage your relationship with the publication's competitors, who may decide not to cover your next announcement. On the other hand, if you work for a global company such as Microsoft or Nike, an exclusive may not damage your relationships at all. Because your news is seen as highly significant, the media doesn't have the luxury of ignoring it for risk of being scooped by competitors. Even if you occasionally grant an exclusive to one publication, the others will continue to cover your company's news. The reality is they have to in order to remain competitive.

SETTING COVERAGE EXPECTATIONS

After each important interview, the PR person should provide a recap to key executives summarizing how the interview went and, if relevant, explaining the organization's vulnerabilities. If the interview didn't go well, we usually send an e-mail saying something like, "I want to let you know that Joe had a really tough interview today. He did the best he could, but here's where we ran into some problems. I want to give you a heads-up that this is the angle the reporter is taking, and I think the headline may be this, and here's what we're doing. If you have any ideas between now and three p.m. today, please let me know because I'm doing everything in my power to head this in a different direction." Providing recaps like this is critical because it allows you to set expectations and eliminate surprises.

Forging better relationships with the media is one of the key ways to take PR to a more strategic level. In Principle 8, we'll show you how to keep the information flowing inside and outside the company once your PR plan is in the implementation stage and the media starts covering your news.

MAINTAIN AN OPEN INFORMATION FLOW

You've got your PR plan. You've successfully lined up interviews with the media. So now the work is done, and you can sit back and relax, right? Well, not exactly. In fact, just the opposite is true. The implementation stage is one of the most critical times for every PR program, requiring people in the organization to pay close attention, think creatively, and be flexible enough to change direction on a dime.

It's important to keep the information flowing inside and outside the organization so you become aware of changes as quickly as they occur. Without this open information flow, employees may end up spending time on issues that are no longer relevant, costing your company precious time and resources. It's also critical to pay attention to the reaction of the media and the marketplace to your announcements so you can make modifications as needed. Otherwise, even the best PR plan can quickly derail.

ANTICIPATING PROBLEMS BEFORE THEY HAPPEN
As you roll out your PR plan, you need to think on your feet. Factors change unexpectedly, requiring you to constantly modify your PR plan as you execute it. So what are some of the scenarios that could throw your PR plan off track?

- *Delays in timing.* The launch of the product may be delayed because a supplier hasn't delivered a part. Or perhaps key executives are out of the office, preventing you from obtaining internal approvals on your materials as quickly as you need them. Or maybe third-party endorsements of your product or service aren't available on schedule, forcing you to delay an announcement.
- *Stalled partner deals.* Perhaps the partnership deal gets delayed, forcing you to push back the announcement. Or maybe the partnership deal falls through, requiring that you rethink your strategy.
- *Lost opportunities.* A competitor may trump your news with a more important story, monopolizing the time of reporters who would have otherwise covered your announcement. Or perhaps a natural disaster or a national crisis occurs, burying your news or leading reporters to ignore it altogether.
- *Product and service problems.* Your product may have a defective part, forcing your organization to recall it. Or perhaps you didn't attract the funding you anticipated, requiring your company to regroup.
- *Weak story angle.* Your product or service may not be as well-received by the media as your organization anticipated, compelling you to sweeten the news or beef up the product or service.
- *Internal crisis.* Perhaps you need to lay off employees, or another crisis unexpectedly happens within your organization, driving your organization into reactive mode while putting your PR plan on hold.

When things change unexpectedly, everyone in the organization, including executives, the PR team, and employees, has a key role to play to ensure that the PR plan stays on track. Executives need to communicate openly as new developments occur and make themselves available to the PR team and to the media. The PR team must consider the implications of every change that occurs and respond in the most strategic way possible. Employees can support the organization's PR efforts by sharing their perspectives, identifying new opportunities, and passing on competitive information as soon as they learn of it.

THE ROLE OF THE EXECUTIVE
A key role for executives during the implementation stage is to provide timely approvals. If you receive a press release or other materials from your PR team, don't let them sit. If you need clarity, ask. Approving materials in a timely manner is critical to a successful PR program. By working ahead of time rather

than waiting until the last minute, you can prevent expensive and senseless mistakes that can easily be avoided.

A strategic executive will also communicate expected slips in the schedule or anticipated changes in messaging before they occur in order to reset expectations. If there's a chance something may slip, the executive should tell the PR team, "Hey, there's the possibility of this happening. Have you all thought through what we should do if it does?" That may sound pretty basic, but the reality is that executives tend to get busy and are in the habit of sharing things only on an absolute need-to-know basis. They may believe it isn't an issue until it actually happens. Or they may view information as power, purposely keeping it from others as a way to keep themselves in the know. By failing to communicate, however, they're preventing their PR team from being fully informed and prepared to execute accordingly. Communicating potential shifts before they happen enables the organization to prepare for changes further in advance, making it possible to take the most strategic action available.

During the implementation stage, the executive should make media interviews a priority, adhere to the scheduled interview times, and take the time to answer inquiries promptly. We've seen executives cancel media interviews after they've been scheduled or push them off onto less knowledgeable executives within the company. As discussed in Principle 7, developing a good rapport with the media is one of the most effective strategies a company can do to promote its message. Scheduling and then canceling media interviews erodes trust and damages the relationship as well as the credibility of the company.

While some executives don't make media interviews a priority, we've also encountered executives who want to capture the entire media spotlight for themselves even when others in the company may be better equipped to serve as the spokesperson on certain topics. Perhaps they feel competitive with their colleagues. Or maybe they see it as their job. Ask yourself if you're the best person to do the interview. If not, make recommendations as to who can attract the best coverage for your company.

THE ROLE OF THE PR TEAM

During the implementation stage, the PR team needs to set clear expectations with executives for a time frame for approval of materials. Clearly communicating deadlines and emphasizing the importance of complying with them can go a long way toward obtaining timely feedback.

As you roll out the PR plan, it's important to keep executives informed about the materials that will be sent out and the relationship of these materials to the organization's broader strategy. "If someone just sends me a press release, that's not really helpful because I'm not sure what the strategy is or the messages I'm supposed to convey," says Michelle Goldberg, a partner at the venture capital firm Ignition Partners. "It's much better to approach people at the board level and say, 'Here's the messaging, here's the press release, and here are the questions we could potentially get and how to answer them.'"

With the help of others in the company, a good PR team also must anticipate changes and proactively plan for them before they occur. PR professionals must constantly ask themselves the question "In the event of the plan changing, what are we going to do?" They must always think analytically, determine the implications of every new development, and communicate the challenges they encounter in a timely manner to the executive team. As you do this, it's important to come to the table with solutions, not just problems. Don't just talk about what's slipped and the problems this is creating. Think through the potential solutions, and be prepared to provide recommendations for moving forward given the new circumstances.

Along the same lines, the PR team should also provide progress reports to the executive team, functional managers, and other company stakeholders. At a minimum, the PR team should provide regular coverage recaps. In addition, the PR team should communicate unanticipated developments, good and bad, as they happen. For example, if a prominent publication writes a highly positive story, send an e-mail summary with a link to the story. Likewise, if a TV station takes a controversial approach to your announcement, communicate that immediately and recommend any actions to be taken.

Managing PR at a Nonprofit

The following is an interview with Dean R. Owen, director of executive communications for international humanitarian organization World Vision.

Q: What are some of the differences between doing PR work for a nonprofit compared with a for-profit company?

Dean R. Owen: With a nonprofit organization, one has the challenge of seeking journalists' interest in issues as opposed to products or services. Every pitch must pass the "So what?" test, which is especially difficult for an international humanitarian organization at a time when many Americans have little interest in or awareness of most of the issues we are pitching. The exception, of course, is during a major natural disaster, such as the 2004 tsunami, when news organizations were clamoring for news and information about our organization's response. In addition, nonprofits do not have quarterly earnings reports or, in most instances, interesting potential mergers, such as Microsoft and Yahoo, or United Airlines and Delta, which have a greater impact on individuals' lives and pocketbooks.

Q: What role does PR play in the World Vision marketing mix?

Owen: The media relations team at World Vision works closely with marketing, especially during a major natural disaster and during seasonal-related fundraising efforts. Those include the 30 Hour Famine, in which teens fast for thirty hours to raise funds and the holiday season gift catalog, when people select "alternative gifts" for their loved ones, such as buying a goat for a poor family instead of a new tie or jewelry. Our promotional efforts help raise World Vision's profile with the public and drive people to our Web site to learn more about a disaster or to examine the gift catalogue items for sale.

Q: In what ways does World Vision use PR to achieve its business objectives?

Owen: One of our major business objectives is to raise the public profile of World Vision. Even though we have been in existence since 1950 and have more than thirty thousand staff in nearly one hundred countries, our name awareness in the U.S. typically is lower than we would like. Extensive media coverage helps to raise that awareness, particularly during a disaster response, when the awareness level spikes then drops down again when the media coverage subsides. In between disasters, we try to raise awareness by placing news and feature stories in major print, broadcast, and Web media outlets.

Q: How do you work to build support for PR within your organization, and why is this important?

Owen: It's very important. In media relations, we see ourselves as a service organization to a range of clients internal to World Vision, from advocacy and government relations staff seeking to move legislation through Congress to the fundraisers striving to increase donations. The degree to which we are effective in our jobs is commensurate with the quality of the relationships we have with internal subject matter experts. If, for example, I've offended our disaster response specialist and he's too busy to return a call from a *New York Times* reporter, I've failed—both the expert and the *New York Times.*

Q: If you're rolling out your PR plan or carrying out a campaign, how do you go about communicating with executives and employees in your organization?

Owen: We're fortunate to have senior leaders who understand the importance of media coverage in building name and brand awareness. Communications has a prominent seat at the leadership table of World Vision. We keep employees up-to-date via an intranet system and through presentations at staff meetings and other forums. Our employees appreciate the demands the media relations team faces, especially during disaster response, and are very supportive and encouraging.

Q: What kinds of communication crisis work does World Vision do?

Owen: World Vision is quite effective in managing crises to our reputation. As we all recognize, a nonprofit's credibility to the public, its donors, and other stakeholders is invaluable. Credibility is currency, and if you squander it, you have nothing. Periodically, bad news about humanitarian agencies receives global attention, such as aid workers or U.N. peacekeepers abusing children. In those instances, we have child protection experts prepared to explain to journalists the steps World Vision takes to prevent this from happening as well as outline our sixty years of work in the developing world.

Q: To be strategic, companies need to develop great relationships with the media. What do you believe are the key factors required to accomplish this?

Owen: Too many people in PR believe it is all about them individually or the company or organization they work for. They focus inwardly then try to identify story ideas to offer journalists. They have it backward. We see ourselves as a resource for journalists, and in turn, we work to develop and nurture relationships with reporters who cover our issues, whether it's international aid, corporate social responsibility, or charitable giving. We identify their interests and needs then look inwardly to World Vision to identify ways to help meet their needs.

Second, as with any organization or profession, World Vision and international humanitarian agencies have their own lingo and acronyms. In my media training sessions with staff, I insist they speak in seventh-grade English. I tell them to pretend they're talking to their mother. Journalists have the responsibility to communicate to their audiences in a clear and concise manner. If our spokespeople cannot communicate clearly and concisely, World Vision probably will not be included in the story—and the journalist might think twice about contacting us in the future.

Q: Does World Vision use blogs, podcasts, social network sites, or other Web 2.0 technologies to reach its audiences in non-traditional ways? How successful have these efforts been?

Owen: Yes, especially in reaching out to younger audiences on advocacy issues. The efforts, thus far, have enjoyed some success in building coalitions to support our campaigns to help influence members of Congress on issues such as child soldiers in Africa or AIDS awareness, education, and prevention programs.

THE ROLE OF EMPLOYEES

Employees also have a role to play during the implementation stage. They can be your biggest ambassadors if they buy into what the company is doing. Openly sharing information with employees encourages them to express their point of view, pass on competitive information, and identify opportunities you may not have thought about. Keeping employees in the know is also a great way to maximize employee morale and align the company in a single direction.

"Internal communication is an area that deserves thoughtful consideration," says Lee Weinstein, principal of Lee Weinstein & Associates and former director of global corporate communications at Nike. "It's important to make sure employees know what you're doing and why. They want to be educated and engaged. If you're launching a great campaign or getting great press, employees want to share in that. It's something that gets them excited."

Not only does communicating with employees help to increase employee morale, it also assists in controlling rumors. The rumor mill always churns more quickly in a vacuum of information. If you leave employees in the dark about what's happening, they may blow the information they do have out of proportion, or the wrong message may get out, damaging employee morale and the organization as a whole.

If your company has a large announcement, send an e-mail to employees before the coverage hits, instructing them where to direct media inquiries. If the news involves sensitive information and you're afraid it will leak, at the very least schedule an e-mail to hit their inbox at the same time the announcement is released to the media.

Tegic Communications kept its employees informed by holding weekly lunch meetings that were open to employees at all levels within the organization, according to Don Davidge, the company's former vice president of marketing and sales. Executives would provide updates about various aspects of the company. As part of the meeting, the PR team would give a brief update about recent specific coverage or their conversations with the media.

"I think it helps everybody realize that, hey, what these PR people are doing on the phones and on e-mail is of value and is paying off," Davidge says. "And I think in a start-up environment where you're trying to create something from nothing, people get a kick out of the fact that the work they're doing is getting recognized worldwide."

Similarly, board game maker Cranium, which has been purchased by Hasbro, kept employees in the know by organizing periodic "huddles" at which everyone in the company gathered to share information. At least two of these huddles were focused on PR and word-of-mouth marketing. "It's an educational thing to let employees know what's happening, and it's also a great source of story ideas," says Richard Tait, the company's founder. "Our company fundamentally believed that the best idea wins. We didn't care who had the idea; we just wanted to make sure the best ideas come to light."

Starbucks, which has 172,000 employees worldwide[1], communicates with them through a variety of channels that include e-mail, employee newsletters, the company's internal portal, and messages blasted by phone to employee inboxes. "For the most part, we'll bring all the senior executives together, and they'll agree on a message we want to share with our partners (employees)," says Brad Stevens, Starbucks's former vice president of U.S. marketing. "From there, we'll cascade the message from level to level throughout the organization."

DEALING WITH DISAPPOINTING RESULTS

If the media isn't covering your announcement or giving it the attention you believe it deserves, get on the phone with a few reporters and gently ask them why. If reporters tell you they don't find your news significant, try to find out if there is anything you can do to sweeten the news, perhaps by providing more customers who will talk about your product or by repositioning the news as part of a larger trend. If reporters aren't covering your announcement because a competitor trumped your news by releasing a more important announcement, perhaps you can propose a different angle to capture the attention of another beat reporter within the news organization.

If the media is responding negatively to your announcement, the first thing you need to do is determine the reason. It's one thing if your organization's message is unclear or is being misinterpreted. It's another thing entirely if the message *is* being accurately interpreted but the market simply doesn't see the value of your product or service. To come up with the best solution, you first need to get to the root of the problem.

Over the years, we've found it's usually possible to avoid negative coverage by being prepared and by anticipating and influencing the coverage before it hits. Occasionally, however, we've encountered executives who have been disappointed with the coverage they've received because all of their key messages weren't fully reflected. If this occurs, talk to the reporter to better understand the filter through which she saw the news and why she reported the article the way she did. Then help the executive understand the reporter's perspective, and discuss what could be done the next time to make it a better story. In a way, a PR person's job is like a lawyer's. You need to understand both the journalist's and the executive's perspectives and then try to broker the best solution.

Setting Expectations with the Client

Whether you work for an organization or an outside PR agency, it's important that you clearly communicate the deadlines required to keep the PR plan on track. We all get busy, and it's easy to postpone reviewing materials until the last minute. Doing so, however, pushes everyone into fire drill mode and can put the entire PR program in jeopardy. Clearly communicating when you're going to deliver your work and when you need executives to provide feedback forces everyone to do their best work. Here's a checklist of questions you should ask yourself as you set expectations with the client:

- Have I clearly communicated what I am going to do and when I am going to do it?
- Have I clearly communicated when the client will hear back from me or when I will deliver the work to the client?
- Have I allowed myself enough time to deliver high-quality work? Will someone else on my team be able to review my work before it goes to the client?
- Are we and the client on the same page regarding expected completion date of the work? If the client has different expectations, have I brainstormed with others on my team about ways to meet his needs?
- Have I thought about how this project fits in with or will affect other projects for this client? Do I need to renegotiate other deadlines with this client or with others?
- If for some reason I am concerned about meeting the deadline, have I communicated with my manager or others on my team?
- Have I communicated when I need the client's approval and feedback in order to deliver the completed work?

PREPARING FOR A CRISIS

You've probably heard it said before: every organization should have a crisis management plan. While that's true, crisis communication plans are more critical for some companies than others. If you work for a maker of computer games, for example, the types of crises you may encounter are likely to be less critical than if you're employed by an airline or pharmaceutical company. The amount of energy you should invest in developing a crisis communication plan depends on the line of business you're in.

The Institute for Crisis Management (ICM), a crisis management consultancy, groups the crises that businesses encounter into four broad categories:

- Acts of God (storms, earthquakes, volcanic action, etc.)
- Mechanical problems (ruptured pipes, metal fatigue, etc.)
- Human errors (the wrong valve was opened, miscommunication about what to do, etc.)
- Management decisions or indecisions (the problem is not serious, nobody will find out)

According to ICM, most crises fall into the last category and are the result of management's lack of action when a problem occurs. Eventually the problem turns into a crisis.

To prepare ahead of time for potential crises, evaluate where your organization is most susceptible and develop an appropriate response plan. Research the crises that have befallen similar companies and evaluate what they did right and how they could have responded better. If your line of business is highly susceptible and the stakes are high, we recommend you enlist the help of an outside firm that specializes in crisis communication.

At the very minimum, every organization should make the after-hours phone numbers of all its team members readily available so that key personnel can be reached at home. In addition, companies should develop a broad policy outlining how information will be gathered and how communication will proceed should a crisis occur.

Be Prompt and Truthful in Your Response

If a crisis does happen, it's important to be prompt and truthful in your response. Within months of each other, ChoicePoint and LexisNexis, two national collectors of consumer information, were forced to deal with large data security breaches that affected tens of thousands of consumers. The way each company dealt with the crisis provides an important lesson about what to do—and what not to do—if an unexpected crisis occurs.

ChoicePoint, the first of the two companies to encounter a security breach, waited four months before notifying consumers. Initially the company informed only California residents that their personal data may have been stolen because it was mandated by California state law. Other states were ignored until their attorneys general pressured ChoicePoint for more information. To make things worse, ChoicePoint responded defensively, saying it had done no wrong and had been tricked into selling the consumer data. Only when negative news coverage began to emerge did the company change its story as well as its response. If that weren't bad enough, it eventually came to light that ChoicePoint executives sold millions of dollars of stock between the time the fraud was discovered and when it was announced to the public.[2] Had ChoicePoint had a better crisis communication plan in place, perhaps it could have avoided this fiasco as well as the resulting damage to its reputation.

In comparison, LexisNexis handled its own data security breach in a far better and more strategic manner. The company announced the security breach promptly and openly provided information. It notified all customers that were possibly affected, met with employees to explain the situation, and gave its salespeople a sample Q&A to help them respond to client inquiries about the issue. After observing ChoicePoint's faulty strategy one month earlier, LexisNexis executives acknowledged they had decided to do things differently. "We spent a lot of time going through the media coverage . . . seeing what mistakes they made and what we could do better," Mary Dale Walters, vice president of global marketing and communications for LexisNexis, told *PRWeek*.[3]

Allow Yourself the Time to Gather the Facts

While it's important to respond quickly, it's also critical that you allow yourself enough time to gather the facts. Companies, in their eagerness to respond to a crisis, sometimes make the situation worse by misstating the facts before gathering all the information. Had PepsiCo responded on the spot to reports that syringes were showing up in Diet Pepsi cans across the United States, the company would only have made the situation worse. Instead it researched the allegations to find it was highly unlikely the syringes could have been added anywhere at the company. First, its high-tech production lines clean the cans automatically and send them inverted down a conveyer belt at high speeds where they emerge at the other end filled and capped. Second, complaints were emerging from different areas of the U.S. served by diverse production facilities.

After examining the facts, PepsiCo decided not to issue a recall of its product, instead telling the media that these incidents were occurring outside PepsiCo's control. Although negative reports about PepsiCo spread like wildfire over the next week, it eventually came to light that the reports were a hoax, and the company's reputation rebounded. "Speed is essential, but so is accuracy," Becky Madeira, PepsiCo's vice president of public affairs told the Public Relations Society of America after the crisis. "It is very dangerous to attempt to explain the cause of the crisis without facts that are corroborated from outside experts. In our cases, the expert was the FDA."[4]

Paying close attention and being prepared to shift gears as you roll out your PR plan will take you a long way toward obtaining the coverage you seek. Once your PR program is fully under way, the next step is measuring its effectiveness and using the results to improve your PR program over time. In Principle 9, we show you how to measure your success and showcase your results to key stakeholders within the organization.

MEASURE AND MERCHANDIZE YOUR RESULTS

As Winston Churchill once said, "However beautiful the strategy, you should occasionally look at the results." Unless you measure the results of your PR program, you can't tell if your efforts are working. What's more, you have no way of knowing whether you're using your time wisely and spending your PR dollars efficiently.

A strategic approach to PR requires knowing what metrics exist and how to use them to measure your success over time. It also involves showcasing your results to key stakeholders so they better understand how PR is helping the organization achieve its most important business objectives.

Historically, PR has been viewed as "soft" and has been kept on the periphery because PR professionals have failed to demonstrate its value in a measurable way. As PR gains greater acceptance in the overall marketing mix, pressure has mounted to find accurate ways to measure the results. Let's face it: the language of business is dollars. Executives want to see evidence that the money they're spending is translating into increased revenue. As discussed in Chapter One, PR can shift the perception of your product, build awareness of your company, and increase the perceived value of your stock. But to foster an understanding of the benefits of PR, it's paramount that you measure and showcase its value. If you can demonstrate a return on investment (ROI) and articulate the impact of your activities on the bottom line, it reinforces the significant role PR plays in achieving your organization's goals. It also demonstrates the reasons that PR should be given a seat at the table.

"If you don't measure your results, how can you justify the PR budget for next year?" says Katherine Lagana, vice president of global legal research for LexisNexis. "Since PR is so qualitative, the challenge then becomes agreeing upon what your measurements of success will be."

Over the years we've seen more and more executives request a measurable return on their PR investment. Nevertheless, nearly half of all companies do not set aside money for measurement. According to a recent *PRWeek*-Cymfony Corporate Survey, only 51 percent of respondents designate money for measurement, and of those that do, more than half allocate just 1 percent to 5 percent of their overall PR budget.[1] Why do most organizations give measurement such short shrift? Some simply don't know how to do it. Others believe there's no payoff. Still others have the false perception that evaluating PR results requires a large sum of money.

The fact is, it's possible to measure your PR results affordably, and the payoff is big. Although there's no single perfect measurement, using a variety of methods can give your organization a good idea about the effectiveness of your PR programs. Evaluating your PR programs also helps to build the case for PR by making it possible to demonstrate the value you're adding to the business. Without measuring your results, there's no way to evaluate whether PR is advancing your business objectives. And without this proof, PR will continue to be viewed as soft and intangible and will be confined to the backseat when in fact it's one of the most cost-effective marketing initiatives you can use to obtain results for your business.

FIVE WAYS TO MEASURE YOUR SUCCESS

While there's no magic bullet when it comes to evaluating your PR results, several metrics exist that can help you assess the effectiveness of your PR program, from both a quantitative and qualitative perspective. While some require time and money, others are straightforward and can be completed in-house at minimum expense. Here are five commonly used metrics and a description of the benefits and limitations of each:

Return on Impressions

This is a quantitative metric that shows the number of people who potentially read your article and the cost of reaching them. "Return on impressions" is calculated by adding up the total number of readers or viewers of each media outlet in which your news story appears and dividing it by the total dollars spent to secure that coverage. If you spent $10,000 to get a story in a newspaper with a circulation of 2 million readers, for example, the return on impressions would be $10,000 divided by 2 million, or .005 cents per impression.

One of the major benefits of this measurement is that it's easy and affordable to calculate. It also resonates with dollar-conscious executives who want to know what they're getting for their money. The limitation, however, is that it doesn't evaluate the quality of the article you secured, nor does it definitively demonstrate the effect on your customers' behavior of the increased awareness generated by the investment in PR. It simply shows the total number of people who may have been exposed to the article and at what cost.

Ad Value Equivalency

This measurement compares the cost-effectiveness of PR with that of advertising. For television coverage, it's measured by calculating the length of time a spokesperson appears on a particular show and then determining the cost of a similar-length ad during this same segment. For print publications, it's calculated by measuring the total column inches of an article and then comparing the cost of securing that coverage to the cost of running a similar-size ad in the same section of the publication. If it cost your PR team $10,000 to secure a half-page story in a trade publication, for example, and the cost of placing the same-size ad would be $50,000, you can show that the cost of PR was five times as cost-effective as advertising.

Like the return on impressions metric, the "ad value equivalency" metric is a quantitative measure that's easy to calculate and resonates with dollar-conscious executives. It's especially useful if you're trying to make the case for the benefits of PR as compared with advertising. Its shortcoming, however, is that it fails to provide an apples-to-apples comparison. Because editorial coverage is considered more believable than advertising, one could argue that a news story has more value than an ad of similar size. In addition, ads generally don't run on the front page of a publication, making it impossible to find an accurate ad value equivalency for high-profile front-page stories.

Return on Media Impact

This metric shows the impact of your PR campaign on sales of your company's product or service. It's calculated by tracking sales of your product before and after your PR campaign. For example, if sales of your product were at 5,000 widgets per month before the PR campaign started, and sales grew to 15,000 widgets per month at the end of the campaign, you may be able to conclude your PR campaign tripled sales. If your widget sells for $30, and the PR campaign cost $10,000, you can show that your expenses of $10,000 generated $300,000 in incremental revenue.

"Return on media impact" is a powerful measurement if calculated properly because it shows the direct influence of the PR campaign on the bottom line. It's a persuasive measurement for people who are influenced by numbers because it directly demonstrates how PR can increase revenue. Its limitation, however, is that it can be hard to track. If your PR campaign coincides with a sales promotion or advertising campaign, for example, it's difficult to isolate to what degree the PR campaign influenced sales as opposed to these other factors.

Return on Influencers

This is a qualitative metric that measures the effect of a PR campaign on customers' perceptions of your company, product, or service. It's measured by evaluating the attitudes of your target audience before and after the PR campaign to determine how perceptions changed. Using a focus group, phone survey, or Web-based survey, for example, a company could examine its target audience to see what percentage of people are aware of its product before the campaign begins and then conduct another survey after the campaign ends to discover how awareness increased. Similarly, it could survey its target audience to determine whether the campaign increased the percentage of people willing to spend money on its product or service.

One of the key benefits of this measurement is that it's a qualitative metric. It shows not only that your PR campaign reached your customers but also how you reached them. It can provide detailed information about how your target audience perceives your organization or product in advance of the PR campaign, allowing you to fine-tune your strategy even before the PR campaign begins. It also provides detailed information about the impact of your PR campaign, helping you assess the effectiveness of the campaign and what changes to incorporate into future programs.

One of the drawbacks, however, is that perception audits can be expensive and time-consuming to complete. To do it right, it's best to hire an outside firm that knows the best way to phrase the survey questions and reach your target audience. As with the measurement for return on media impact, it's not an exact science. When other initiatives are taking place at the same time, it can be difficult to assess to what degree the PR campaign influenced customer perceptions as compared with these other factors.

Share of Voice

This is a quantitative and a qualitative metric that measures the number of articles published as well as the degree to which an organization's key messages are making their way into news coverage. It also enables an organization to measure the quantity and quality of news coverage as compared with that of its competitors. If you have a three-month PR campaign, for example, you can count the number of articles that were published during that time. In addition, you can assess the number of articles that included your key messages and give an overall rating as to whether the article was positive, negative, or neutral. With a "share of voice" metric, it's also possible to count the number of articles your competitors published during the same period and assess whether your company was positioned favorably against the competition. We usually give each article a rating of from one through four, four being the most favorable to our client's organization.

The share of voice metric offers many benefits. First, it's both quantitative and qualitative, meaning that it allows you to measure the total number of articles as well as how those actual messages are reflected. This helps to give a full picture of the coverage you're receiving. Second, it allows you to measure the quantity and quality of news coverage against your competitors. Finally, it's a measurement that's both practical and affordable, making it convenient to use weekly and monthly. One of the chief limitations, however, is that it doesn't show you the effect of the coverage your organization receives on customer behavior. Nor does it demonstrate the influence of PR on the bottom line.

Measuring Your Results

The following is an interview with Mark Weiner, CEO of PRIME Research North America, an international communications research provider. He is the author of Unleashing the Power of Public Relations: A Contrarian's Guide to Marketing and Communication.

Q: Why is measuring your PR results so important in the current business landscape?

Mark Weiner: Measuring results has always been important in the business landscape; the notion just seems new to people in public relations because, for whatever reason, we in PR have managed to get along without it. We are, however, in a business environment in which the expectation is that everything can be measured, and PR is no exception. Measurement is the means by which one proves value and improves performance.

Proving value is one of PR's greatest challenges but not for those who set measurable objectives, gain agreement from internal clients, and then evaluate their programs based on the agreed-upon objectives. Improving performance is also made easier through measurement. The ongoing process of setting standards and then continuously improving performance by measuring and adjusting against these standards ensures you're in a position to learn and improve before it's too late.

Q: What percentage of organizations currently measure their PR results?

Weiner: Depending on how one defines "measure," the number may be surprisingly high or low. Most PR organizations measure by maintaining activity logs and clip books. The good thing is that the principles behind proving value and improving performance can work with even simple measures such as these. The suggestion here, of course, is that every organization can and should measure.

Q: Why do many companies skip this step?

Weiner: Most organizations skip this important step because they prefer to follow the conventional wisdom. Among the most common myths are that PR can't be measured, that it has to be complicated or expensive, that PR people don't have the necessary technical expertise, that measurement is used strictly as a basis for punishment, and that management and staff won't support PR measurement. Like I said, all of these are myths.

Q: What are the consequences of failing to measure results?

Weiner: While it's been true in my experience that those who embrace PR measurement enjoy the benefits of bigger budgets, greater respect within the organization, professional advancement, and more, I think the worst of all consequences is the dull pain that comes with not knowing where you are, how you're doing, and whether anyone appreciates the PR you're delivering. On an organizational level, measurement guides smarter marketing and communication investment decisions. On that level, the impact of a bad strategy or poorly executed plan can have serious financial repercussions. I've been involved in cases where PR measurement revealed the course of action by which companies have avoided catastrophic costs in the billions of dollars.

Q: Is it possible for companies, particularly small businesses, to measure their results in ways that aren't expensive?

Weiner: People wrongly assume that PR measurement is too expensive or too sophisticated. The simplest, least expensive way to measure is to begin by clearly understanding the role of PR within your or your client's organization, to uncover the expectations and preferences from among the executives who either fund or influence funding of your PR program, and then to "negotiate" objectives that are reasonable, measurable, and meaningful. This process is always productive for ensuring that objectives are aligned with the organization and with expectations. And if simple, inexpensive measures are what is reasonable, then one must ensure that the measures are as meaningful as they can be.

Q: Do you feel it's possible to accurately measure the return on one's PR investment?

Weiner: I do. Let me begin by offering a distinction between "proving value," which I referenced earlier, and "delivering a return on investment," or ROI. Values are subjective from organization to organization and even from person to person within the same organization. ROI, on the other hand, is a financial term which essentially means the amount of money brought into or kept within the organization compared to the level of investment. There are three types of PR ROI in my experience.

The first is doing more with less. While this form of ROI is the most common, most people don't consider "efficiency" to be an ROI driver even though it is. Most people in PR are conscious of targeting press releases and leading with the highest-potential tactics, for example. The only limitation is that this form of ROI has the lowest yield since the resources that can be retained are only a percentage of the existing budget.

The second is *making the PR-to-sales connection.* New forms of marketing and communications analytics are helping leading-edge organizations to connect the various elements of the marketing and communication mix to sales and even stock price. They are using sophisticated statistical models that track the presence of a particular form of marketing, including PR, within a particular market at a particular time. Over the course of a year, certain patterns emerge when the marketing tracking is compared to sales data market by market and week by week. These analyses, commonly called marketing mix models, eventually associate a certain sales contribution to each marketing element. The great news for PR is that it routinely delivers the best ROI of any marketing and communication agent.

The third form of PR ROI is *avoiding catastrophic cost.* People have often asked, "How do you measure the quality of good counsel?" One way is to measure a crisis avoided. And while linking PR to sales has always held the highest sex appeal, catastrophic cost is where the biggest impact of PR can be felt. For an example of how not to do it, look at how Bridgestone/Firestone and Ford chose to publicly blame each other for the exploding tire debacle earlier this decade: a review of the two companies' stock prices during the very public squabble indicates Ford lost roughly 70 percent of its market capitalization and Bridgestone/Firestone lost about 65 percent.[7] Think of the many shareholders, retirees, and employees holding stock in these companies and the impact of poor communications on them.

Q: What percentage of the PR budget should companies ideally devote to measurement?

Weiner: For the longest time I've heard people say that 10 percent for research is the right number. I disagree. Research budgets depend on a variety of factors, not the least of which is what the organization or brand is trying to accomplish. For example, if your brand is dying and the company is simply milking it for whatever it can squeeze out of it, then I would recommend a very low level of research investment. If, on the other hand, you are the PR lead for the next iPhone, 10 percent may not be enough considering the high stakes involved. The simple but often frustrating answer to the PR research allocation question is, "It depends."

Q: What are some of the biggest mistakes you see companies make as they try to measure their PR results?

Weiner: There are two types of mistakes: the intentional and the unintentional. Among the most severe intentional mistakes in my opinion is the use of what I'll call PR multipliers and other unfounded compounding effects. I've heard people argue that because PR is more credible than advertising that the PR value should be multiplied. Then arbitrary factors are used to multiply everything from ad values to circulation and more. It's voodoo math, and my advice to any PR client when confronted with multipliers is to learn how to divide.

Unintentional mistakes might include not doing your homework before investing in the first place. Outside research firms can be expensive, and one has a responsibility to ask for and check references. It's also a mistake in my opinion to invest in research without first aligning your PR objectives within the organization since you may be focusing on the wrong measure.

Q: What advice do you have for PR people who want to measure their results but don't know where to start?

Weiner: There's a lot of free information available, and I would suggest to anyone interested in undertaking a PR research program to begin there. One great source is the Institute for Public Relations, which offers free white papers and opinion pieces on the subject of PR research. Go to www.instituteforpr.org to access some of the best insights available anywhere. There are also some excellent books available and a number of PR measurement blogs.

Beyond doing your homework, my advice is simply to measure your results. The benefits from this are so great. I know of no executive who would find fault in someone wanting to improve his or her performance. Simple measures are better than no measures. I'd rather be half-right than totally in the dark. Measure whether you're asked to or not. Introduce measurement thinking to your PR department and to leading executives. Eventually they will begin to appreciate the effort as you show that even a simple measurement system yields insights, value, and the basis for continual improvement.

DECIDING WHICH MEASUREMENTS TO USE

The measurements you should use depend on your budget and your desired business objectives. Thinking strategically about your goals will help to clarify which measurements make the most sense. If your goal is to increase sales, for example, you may want to measure return on impact. If your goal is to boost awareness of your product or service, you may want to use the return on influencers metric. If you're trying to convince your CFO about the cost-effectiveness of PR as compared with advertising, you may want to measure ad value equivalency. If you want to measure how your organization is viewed in comparison with your competitors, you may want to use share of voice.

If your company has a limited budget, our recommendation is that you measure, at a minimum, return on impressions and share of voice. This will enable you to engage in some discussion about the return on your PR investment. It will also make it possible to demonstrate the quantity of coverage you're obtaining as well as the degree to which your key messages are resonating with the media.

While none of these measurements is an exact science, they can have a huge impact on the direction of your PR program. For example, over the years, PricewaterhouseCoopers (PwC) has used share of voice measurements to convince executives to spend more money on PR. The PR team develops quarterly reports that monitor the percentage of negative and positive stories, tracks journalists that regularly write about PwC, and identifies strategies that lead to favorable media coverage. By closely monitoring its results, the PR team was able to determine that press coverage increased when the company accompanied a press release with a graph or chart. In addition, it determined which reporters and publications wrote most often about the accounting industry, allowing the PR team to hone its media strategy. The PR team also realized it obtained more favorable coverage when making the CEO available to talk to the media, helping it to convince the CEO to make himself available for more press interviews.

"Our research of the effectiveness of a public relations program swept away management's subjective negativism such as 'Why aren't we getting press,' when of course we had been," Peter Horowitz, senior managing director for global public relations at PwC, said in a PR measurement report issued by the Council of Public Relations Firms. "I had been fighting the battle for twenty years, but now I have definitive proof of public relations' effectiveness, and it has changed the way our management views what we do."[2]

Similarly, Sears enlisted measurement vendor Delahaye Medialink to help it use the return on influencers measurement to gauge consumers' view of the company before and after they saw Oprah Winfrey announce its donation of $20,000 worth of Christmas gifts to needy families. The survey showed a fivefold increase in consumer perceptions that Sears does good things for the community and the environment. Those who expressed their intent to shop at Sears increased from 59 percent to 70 percent, and estimated spending levels rose 39 percent per shopper, translating into a return of investment of $13 million in potential sales.[3] By measuring its results, Sears was able to clearly show that one prominent placement can transform customer attitudes and lead to millions of dollars in additional revenue.

How often you evaluate your PR program depends on your business objectives, the length of your campaign, and the measurements you use. Because of its cost, the return on influencer metric is something you might want to invest in only once a year, before and after a critical PR campaign. On the other hand, the share of voice metric is a measurement you can conduct weekly or monthly, tracking trends over time. The return on impressions, ad value equivalency, and return on media impact metrics can be calculated over specific time periods or at the end of a significant campaign. Whatever measurements you decide to use, you should outline them in advance within your PR plan so that everyone understands from the start how you plan to evaluate your success.

GETTING STARTED

As PR people, many of us know we should be measuring our results. But with so much time taken up by the development and implementation of PR programs, we often don't make the time. If no one at the C-level is demanding that results be measured, we never quite get to it even though we know we should; and this, in turn, creates low-level stress. In their book *You: Staying Young*, Dr. Michael Roizen and Dr. Mehmet Oz argue that the most damaging type of stress doesn't result from an immediate crisis or a major tragedy such as the loss of a loved one; it's the constant nagging feeling you get when you're avoiding things you ought to be doing over long periods of time.[4]

For many people, the failure to measure PR results creates low-level stress. Not knowing if your efforts are working or if you're spending your money wisely creates an uneasy feeling. It also prevents you from properly fine-tuning your programs as you go. It's not so important how much money you devote to measurement; what's critical is that you take a few small steps to start the process. Maybe you decide you're simply going to familiarize yourself with the types of measurements you can use. Or maybe you ask a coordinator on your team to pull together a list of articles placed over the last twelve months and begin to analyze the messages reflected in those articles. A few small steps will get the ball rolling and will do wonders for the quality of your PR programs. Once you get started, you can always expand your measurement program by adding more sophisticated evaluation techniques later on.

"We have created a simple but valuable quarterly report to measure results," says Harvey Bauer, marketing manager with Tideworks Technology. "Our report summarizes the number of press releases distributed, the number of articles published, total costs, and total impressions. By looking at these four things quarterly over the last several years, we have gained insight into the effectiveness of specific PR activities."

BUDGETING FOR MEASUREMENT

Measuring your results doesn't have to cost a lot. As a general rule, we recommend allocating at least 5 percent or more of your overall PR budget to measurement. Of course, that percentage will vary depending upon the overall size of your company, your PR budget, and the complexity of your campaigns. "Whether it's 10 percent or 2 percent, the PR budget and the research budget should not be in lockstep: expenditures should vary with the organization's needs at a given time," Mark Weiner, CEO of PRIME Research North America, writes in his book, *Unleashing the Power of PR*. "For example, a mature brand with a huge PR budget may require only a fraction of 1 percent whereas a category-redefining significant new product roll-out may justify spending 10 percent or more during the initial phases."[5]

The budget for a measurement program typically involves the cost of tracking articles plus the labor required to calculate your results using the metrics you choose. The Internet makes available many online services that will track coverage free of charge. Using Google or Technorati, for example, you can type in keywords and have coverage sent to you regularly. You can also subscribe to a news monitoring service, such as Cision or PR Newswire, which will monitor your news coverage for a flat monthly rate.

The labor required to measure your results is usually just a few hours a week or a month, depending on how much coverage you attract and which coverage you choose to analyze. Companies with larger budgets sometimes hire outside measurement vendors to conduct perception audits, analyze share of voice, and measure their results using proprietary models. For example, vendors such as Delahaye Medialink, PR Trak, Biz360, and Cision use sophisticated formulas to track the quantity and quality of coverage and relate it back to a company's bottom line. We recommend you work closely with any outside vendor you might choose so you fully understand the analysis and can make the best recommendations to your clients.

The PR team at Deloitte uses Cision to track its share of voice every month so that it can determine whether the company is "moving the needle" as compared with its competitors in the accounting and consulting space. Using a proprietary formula, the tracking service measures the tonality, prominence, message pickup, and frequency of coverage in various competitors, giving Deloitte an overall score against each of its competitors.

The Deloitte PR team shares this data with senior executives to support their efforts and also to bolster its argument for additional PR resources. "I'm a strong believer that you have to measure what you're doing," says Keith Lindenburg, director, national public relations, Deloitte Services LP. "You can talk about value, but at the end of the day people want to see the numbers, and that's what we're showing them."

On occasion, the Nike PR team has used the return on media impact metric to measure the effect of news stories on sales. For example, when Nike released its line of digital sport watches, the PR team developed a plan that included pitching a story to *Wired* magazine. Thanks to this story placement, the sport watches sold out the first season they were introduced, according to Lee Weinstein, principal of Lee Weinstein & Associates and Nike's former director of global corporate communications. Because no other marketing efforts were developed to promote the product, the PR team was able to measure the direct impact of its news coverage on sales.

"That was a campaign where we could directly measure the ROI of PR," says Weinstein. "The fact that there were no competing marketing initiatives gave us direct insight into the value of PR. That made it such a great campaign."

MERCHANDIZING YOUR RESULTS

As you measure your results, it's important to share them with key stakeholders, which often include the executive team, the board of directors, and investors. A great way to showcase your results is to display them in graph form over a period of time to illustrate how the data is trending. If the return on impressions goes down from fifteen cents to five cents over a three-month period, for example, demonstrating this through a graph helps to showcase this trend. Similarly, bar graphs are an effective way to display the quantity of your organization's coverage as compared with that of your competitors. Graphing your results enables you to better explain the significance behind the numbers, providing a level of perspective that doesn't show up when presenting the numbers in raw form.

COST PER IMPRESSION

	Month 1	Month 2	Month 3
Impressions	2,000,000	5,000,000	10,000,000
PR Spend	$ 10,000	$ 15,000	$ 20,000
Cost Per Impression	$ 0.0050	$ 0.0030	$ 0.0020

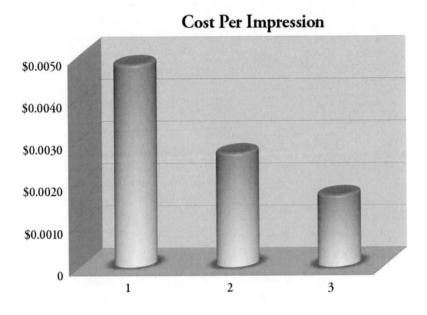

Cost Per Impression

SHARE OF VOICE

	Company 1	Company 2	Company 3	Company 4
News articles (Oct. 22-Nov. 22)	31	12	16	15
Blog Mentions (Oct. 22-Nov. 22)	273	102	101	84
Technorati Results	1,581	622	733	5,136
Press Releases	2	3	1	1

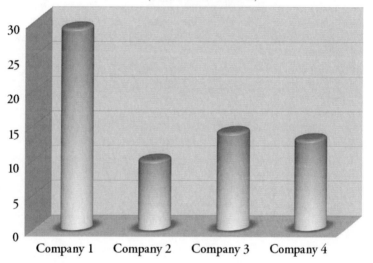

News Articles
(October 22 –November 22)

In addition to showcasing your measurement results, you'll want to share the actual coverage your organization receives with key internal company stakeholders. As discussed in Principle 8, it's important to send executives significant news stories—good and bad—as soon as they appear. In addition, you'll want to provide significant coverage recaps either weekly or monthly. If you use the share of voice measurement, these recaps should include an overall summary explaining the coverage you received during the time period, a brief summary of the messages included in each story, a numerical rating of the coverage, and a link to each full-length story.

A good way to get more mileage out of your positive coverage is to showcase it to a broader audience that may include employees, job candidates, customers, partners, and the public at large. If you secure a great article, frame it and hang it in your lobby, conference room, or even next to the cash register. Write a blog about it. Highlight it on the careers and news sections of your Web site. E-mail it to employees, partners, your board of directors, and customers, and provide it to job candidates as part of their information packet. You can also develop books showcasing your company's clips over a longer time period, display them in the lobby, give them to key company stakeholders, and provide them to potential recruits. Merchandising your results like this allows you to promote your company in a significant way while reinforcing the value PR provides.

John Wanamaker, considered by many to be the father of advertising, once said, "I know that half of my advertising dollars are wasted. I just don't know which half."[6] In today's business world, companies don't have the luxury of wasting half their budget, let alone a quarter. Consistently measuring and merchandising your results will help ensure that your organization spends its PR dollars in the most strategic way possible. It also reinforces the critical role PR plays in moving your business forward.

KEEP YOUR PR PROGRAM RELEVANT OVER TIME

No matter how strategic your initial PR program, it will eventually fall dead in its tracks if business conditions change and it ceases to be relevant. As with any plan, it's important to revisit your PR program over time to make sure it remains completely up-to-date with your organization's overall business objectives and the external climate.

Maintaining the relevance of your PR program involves holding periodic post mortems to discuss your results and then making the changes needed to improve the PR program over time. It also requires keeping your PR acumen current so you continue to reach your audiences in the most relevant way.

THE POST MORTEM

In the spirit of continuous improvement, you should get into the habit of holding post mortems to discuss what went well with your latest PR campaign and what didn't. The purpose of post mortems is to capture best practices for use in the future. Post mortems provide a chance to gather feedback from all the key stakeholders and to use that information to grow and evolve. They allow your organization to address issues head-on rather than sweeping them under the rug. They also help you understand the perspectives of all the participants, enabling you to rebuild consensus and once again align the team in a common direction.

While post mortems are essential to any strategic PR program, our experience is that organizations frequently skip them. In some cases, PR practitioners are running so fast that it's difficult to make the time to stop and reflect. In other cases, they're reluctant to open up their work to potential criticism from senior managers. Simply put, they're afraid to expose their mistakes and shortcomings.

But if you don't hold post mortems, you don't learn; and if you don't learn, it's impossible to strengthen your PR program over time. Without full access to information, you might mistakenly assume that the executive team was happy with the results or that an initiative worked when it actually failed. It may not be a huge organizational issue at the moment, but if people don't believe that their voices are heard, over time the problems will fester. Eventually you may lose the business or even your job.

We recently held a post mortem with one of our clients after a major announcement. During the discussion, the CEO commented that the announcement had been successful but asked us if there had been anything we wished we had done differently. One thing that had worked well was tying the news to a larger trend, which helped us to capture a large volume of coverage, all of it positive. In addition, the company's executives were well-prepared for interviews and did an excellent job delivering their messages to the media. But on greater reflection, we concluded that we would have been more successful persuading certain bloggers and trade publication editors to write about the announcement had we reached out to them further in advance.

By holding a post mortem, we were able to identify additional opportunities we could begin to cultivate immediately. In addition, the post mortem helped us to forge a deeper relationship with our clients by listening to their feedback and showing them we really do care. We weren't just checking the box to say we completed the PR plan but were truly interested in brainstorming ways that we could strengthen our PR program over time.

ASKING THE RIGHT QUESTIONS

Organizations should hold post mortems every time they've completed a major campaign or initiative. This could be after the completion of a press tour, a major trade show, or a press conference. Typically, all key stakeholders should be invited: the PR team, the CEO, the senior management team, and any spokespeople who participated in the campaign.

The post mortem provides a great opportunity to share your measurable results (see Principle 9) and your strategy that led to these results. It also provides a chance to ask a set of strategic questions that will help you improve your PR program over time. These are among the questions we often pose during post mortems:

- Did we achieve our business objectives?
- How valuable was the coverage in helping us to achieve our business objectives?
- Where did we shine? What could we have done better?
- Were any of the implemented tactics problematic?
- How effective were the spokespeople?
- Were there any significant obstacles that had to be overcome?
- Did the value of the program merit the cost?

Presenting a set of open-ended questions will allow you to gather the spectrum of feedback needed to strengthen your PR program the next time around. It will also expose where opinions diverge, helping you to realign stakeholders and reunite them in a common direction.

TIPS FOR MAKING THE POST MORTEM A SUCCESS

Like any productive business meeting, a successful post mortem requires the right ground rules, timing, and approach. Here are six tips to help you make the meeting a success:

1. *Be strategic about whom you include.* Before scheduling the post mortem, think through your method for soliciting the most candid information and steps that will work best to align the team. If various team members are likely to have different opinions, you may want to hold a formal meeting with the entire team in the same room. If it's difficult to obtain candid feedback in a group setting, you may want to take a softer approach and organize informal meetings with one key stakeholder at a time.

2. *Meet informally with stakeholders in advance.* Even if you decide to schedule a formal meeting, it's often a good idea to meet one-on-one with all the key stakeholders beforehand. Meeting individually with each participant in advance of the post mortem creates a safe environment for each person to offer candid feedback. It also provides a heads-up about the issues that are likely to come up in the more formal meeting of the entire group, allowing you to prepare in advance.

3. *Be strategic about the timing.* It's best to allow some time to pass after the PR campaign ends before scheduling the post mortem. The day after a campaign, people may feel tired and burnt out. By allowing more time to pass, you let people recuperate, gain some distance, and reflect on the campaign before giving feedback. On the other hand, if you let too much time pass, people will have moved on to other initiatives, will feel too removed, and won't want to take the time to debrief.

4. *Carefully select who leads the meeting.* To ensure the success of the post mortem, it's critical to select someone to lead the meeting more removed than the PR person responsible for the day-to-day execution. The best facilitator is someone who's familiar with the objectives of the campaign but wasn't working on it every day. Selecting the right person to lead the meeting will help keep emotional commentary at a minimum, making it easier for participants to candidly share their comments.

5. *Create a safe environment for sharing feedback.* To get the post mortem off to a good start, it's important to set the ground rules upfront. Be aware that many people are uncomfortable giving and receiving candid feedback, and try to make the meeting environment a safe one. Emphasize that everyone worked hard and that the intent of the debriefing is neither to shower each other with kudos or place blame but rather to learn what worked and what didn't. The more that people feel free to communicate openly, the better the PR program will become in the long run. It's also critical that everyone listen openly without getting defensive or argumentative. To provide genuine feedback, people need to know that the participants can keep emotion out of the mix.

6. *Keep it solution-focused.* Along the same lines, it's important to create a meeting format that focuses on solutions, not just problems. If a person discusses something that didn't go well, ask him how the situation could be handled differently in the future. By getting the group to brainstorm solutions, the facilitator helps ensure that the post mortem won't deteriorate into a venting session.

   It's important to point out here that when someone raises a problem, they want to know how it's going to be fixed. As an example, we rented a vacation home over the holidays, only to discover after we arrived that the oven didn't work. This created a problem for us because we couldn't cook our turkey or any other holiday meals. When we called the manager's office, all we kept hearing was, "Sorry, sorry, sorry."

   When something goes wrong, you don't really care if the person's sorry. You want to know what he or she is going to do about it. Is the person going to come over and fix the oven? Is he going to lower the price of the vacation rental? The same logic applies to post mortems. If someone raises an issue, make sure you reach consensus about how it will be fixed next time.

By the end of the post mortem, you should have obtained a detailed view of people's thoughts about the campaign, what worked well and what didn't, and what actions need to be taken moving forward. Write up a summary of what was discussed and share it with all the participants. Include a list of your key takeaways from the discussion and your plans to address any problems that arose during the campaign.

Executives in a variety of industries say they continually evaluate their PR programs to keep them relevant over time. For example, game maker Cranium, Inc. (which has since been bought by Hasbro) held two strategy sessions every year, one to evaluate the previous year's PR plan and one to set new strategy for the coming year, according to Richard Tait, the company's founder. "The media environment was so dynamic that it was critical to go back and evaluate whether we were on the right course," he says. "We needed to constantly be asking, 'Are we where we need to be?'"

Similarly, accounting and consulting firm Deloitte constantly evaluates and refreshes its PR programs. "We may have developed an elaborate campaign, but perhaps nobody was interested, so we'll sit down, reevaluate, and try to come up with another creative approach that people find compelling and interesting," says Keith Lindenburg, director, national public relations, Deloitte Services LP. "You can't be complacent. You always have to be looking at continual improvement."

IF YOU'RE NOT GETTING THE EXPECTED RESULTS

So what should you do if you're not getting the results you expected? Say you're a company executive who's working with an internal PR team, or you're a marketing director who hired an outside PR agency. The PR campaign is over, and you're not satisfied with the coverage. Perhaps your PR team wasn't able to get your organization the media coverage you expected. Or perhaps the quality of coverage was less than optimal. What should you do?

First, don't wait for your PR team to suggest a post mortem. Schedule one yourself. Although people have a tendency to wait with bad news, it's important to organize a meeting immediately and share your concerns. Most PR teams want to do great work. If the way they're executing a plan doesn't match your expectations, give them a chance to change.

In addition, share your concerns candidly. Although it's hard to give feedback, doing so directly and honestly is critical. If you don't share your concerns, the relationship will deteriorate because you're not being honest. As you provide feedback, keep the conversation focused on shared expectations. What did you agree on in the PR plan? How did the results measure up? Listen openly to your PR team's perspective. What went wrong? Why do they feel they weren't able to get the results you agreed on? Finally, evaluate what you could be doing differently. Questions to ask yourself include these:

- Are we properly funding the program?
- Have we given it enough time for our desired results to emerge?

- Are we providing timely feedback?
- Are we giving our PR team access to the right information and people?
- Do we have internal alignment for our objectives?
- Are we setting deadlines that allow the PR team to accomplish its best work?
- Are we doing anything else that negatively affects the PR team's ability to achieve the best results?

Throughout the years, we've found that organizations have a tendency to overreact. When they don't get the results they want, their first thought is to shake things up by changing PR teams. Not only is that an expensive and time-consuming process, it's often unnecessary. In his book *The Tipping Point*, Malcolm Gladwell explains how small changes can have big effects.[1] There's a difference of only one degree between rain and snow, yet the difference is a dramatic one. In the same way, small tweaks can sometimes significantly strengthen a relationship. The challenge is to communicate your concerns candidly, come to agreement over what changes will be made, and then see if these changes materialize over time.

Of course, sometimes it is necessary to cut the cord. If you're an executive and your PR team consistently fails to follow through on the promises you've mutually agreed on, or you're getting signs that the PR team isn't committed to your account, communicate your concerns. If no change occurs, it may be time to end the relationship. Similarly, if you work for a PR agency and your client has unrealistic expectations or isn't giving you the time and resources you need to do a good job, openly communicate your concerns. If the client isn't willing to rectify the problem, it may be time to jump ship.

KEEPING YOUR PR ACUMEN CURRENT

In today's world, the field of public relations is constantly changing and continues to evolve at lightning speed. Phenomena such as online social networking and consumer-generated media are continuing to develop, and these trends are likely to have a profound effect on the PR arena. PR firms are struggling to find ways to engage people online. Many multinational PR agencies are carving out separate practice groups designed to address the rapidly evolving digital landscape.

As the field continues to change, it's critical that executives at all levels of the company keep their PR acumen current so they can fully leverage the venues their customers turn to for news and entertainment. We recommend that you take these steps to keep abreast of new developments:

- *Read voraciously.* Subscribe to industry publications such as *PRWeek* and *PR News*. Read the *Wall Street Journal*'s "Media & Marketing" section. Glance through industry publications such as *Bulldog Reporter*. Read about industries outside your own for ideas. We keep a PR training folder in which we keep stories sent to us electronically and read them whenever there's downtime.

- *Attend classes and industry meetings.* Industry organizations such as the Public Relations Society of America (PRSA), the International Association of Business Communicators (IABC), and the Association for Women in Communications (AWC) have chapters in many communities across the United States, offering PR professionals the chance to get together and discuss best practices. The *Bulldog Reporter* offers audio conferences that provide the opportunity to learn about trends and strategies from other PR practitioners and journalists. Attending sessions such as these is a great way to keep up with the PR industry as it evolves.

- *Blog about PR practices.* Blogging about PR practices is an effective way to keep up with trends because it forces you to read and internalize information and then develop a point of view. If you're not in a position to blog for your company, develop an internal memo focusing on the latest PR trends and send it to company executives once a quarter. This is a great way to educate yourself and others.

- *Be inquisitive.* Talk to people. Ask questions. Try out new technologies. This will help keep the job interesting while giving you a firsthand understanding of new trends and technologies as they emerge. It will also help you to develop a point of view as to their usefulness in the PR arena.

- *Solicit different points of view.* Establish a process for soliciting different points of view about current PR trends, and use these discussions to establish an organizational perspective. Every company has a unique vantage point and can add value by sharing its perspective with journalists.

The Chinese general and military strategist Sun-Tzu said, "The highest form of generalship is to conquer the enemy by strategy."[2] As PR gains more prominence, a strategic approach will separate the best companies from the average ones, propelling them toward maximum success. We hope the ten principles discussed in this book help you garner the satisfaction and rewards of achieving consistently great results. The time to start harnessing the power of PR is now. We wish you the best as you work to obtain maximum influence for your company.

APPENDIX

HUNSK MOTORCYCLES

C ommuniqué PR developed the following public relations plan for fictitious
company Hunsk Motorcycles. We read an interactive Harvard Business
Review (HBR) case study of this fictitious company[1] and developed the plan to
demonstrate the elements and creative thinking that a good strategic PR plan
should include. HBR's cases, which are fictional, present common corporate
marketing dilemmas.

INTRODUCTION

You'll find our ideas for public relations activities to support Hunsk's business and
communication objectives below. Clearly this is an exciting time for your company,
and there are a number of significant ways in which we can raise awareness of
Hunsk's commitment to producing the world's highest-quality motorcycles.

In this plan we have recapped our understanding of the dynamics in Hunsk's
market as well as reiterated our understanding of who you want to reach and
what messages you need them to hear. We find it valuable to include this
information in our plans because it provides context for our recommendations
for specific strategies and tactics.

Please know that Communiqué PR is fully committed to the success of our
clients, ensuring they receive the highest possible return on their PR investment.
We fully expect to make revisions to this plan based on your feedback and that
of your colleagues. Furthermore, we view plans as living documents that we
continually refer to and refine throughout our relationship.

As we execute the subsequent strategies and tactics outlined below, we expect to gain new insights about what messages are resonating and how we might modify campaigns to be even more successful.

We hope these ideas are helpful, and we look forward to receiving your feedback.

SITUATION ANALYSIS

- Hunsk Motorcycles has been in business for more than twenty years. Its main competitor is Harley-Davidson.
- Hunsk customers are primarily men aged thirty-five to fifty and college educated who view themselves as risk-takers. They want a bike that "ticks like a clock and moves like a rocket."
- Through the first six months of this year, shipments of Hunsk motorcycles were approximately 125,900 units, a 7.2 percent decrease compared to last year's 135,600 units.
- The company anticipates that U.S. economic conditions and ongoing consumer concerns will continue to create challenges at least through the end of the year. Nonetheless, the executive management team remains confident about its future and is committed to managing and reinvesting in the business for the long term.
- The management team recognizes that the Hunsk marketing campaign, with ineffective materials and positioning, is outdated; it's lost its "oomph." The PR and marketing campaigns are not reaching the company's target audience, and the employees promoting its motorcycles don't always have direct experience with the product.
- In the past, Hunsk has updated its marketing campaigns to align with trends in the broader consumer market (younger demographic, eco-friendly business practices, lightweight body and machinery) and in the process has lost touch with its core demographic, neglecting to establish a key message and value proposition that resonated with its customer base.
- The company is interested in getting back to its marketing roots, with a goal to be more authentic. Again, the company's core demographic is men who view themselves as the real rebels. They are fiercely independent, confident, and edgy.

BUSINESS OBJECTIVES

- Boost sales and drive revenue.
- Reconnect with the core customer and recapture market share from competitors.
- Build the perceived value of the company.

COMMUNICATION OBJECTIVES
- Elevate the visibility and value of the brand.
- Deepen relationships with loyal customers and enthusiasts.
- Create a sustainable platform for coverage across a variety of media, positioning Hunsk as the maker of the finest motorcycles in the world.

TARGET AUDIENCES
- Consumers, primarily men aged thirty-five to fifty
- Employees
- Shareholders
- Investors

TARGET MEDIA
- Motorcycle enthusiast publications
- Men's lifestyle and general interest magazines
- National business publications
- Motorcycle and automotive blogs and online communities

KEY MESSAGES
- Hunsk is in the business of making the world's best motorcycles to create exceptional experiences for its customers. The company is committed to innovation as it continues producing great motorcycles.
- The company has the right management team in place and is well poised to position Hunsk for the future, to strengthen its bonds with its current customers, and to secure new customers. The road ahead is looking bright.
- Outstanding corporate governance has been a long-standing business practice at Hunsk because it makes good business sense. Although the motorcycle business is fun, corporate governance is something we take seriously.
- Hunsk understands that its customers don't want to be sold to. They want to be part of the brand and what it represents, which is the freedom, excitement, and adventure of the open road.

STRATEGY OVERVIEW
We have identified the following six strategies that Communiqué PR can implement on behalf of Hunsk Motorcycles. They can be executed in tandem or as disparate projects.

Strategy 1:   Demonstrate Hunsk's value with motorcycle enthusiasts.
Strategy 2:   Tie Hunsk to key lifestyle trends and consumer habits.

Strategy 3:   Tell the story of Hunsk's reinvention and return to its roots.
Strategy 4:   Create support for Hunsk online.
Strategy 5:   Hit the road with museum participation.
Strategy 6:   Pursue and win industry awards.

STRATEGY 1: DEMONSTRATE HUNSK'S VALUE WITH MOTORCYCLE ENTHUSIASTS

To help Hunsk Motorcycles reach its target audience and demonstrate value to them, we recommend placing articles in the magazines read by serious motorcycle enthusiasts. Specifically, we envision targeting journalists with *American Motorcyclist, Easy Riders, Rider*, and others for coverage. Communiqué PR would reach out to editors of these magazines with the goal of reviving awareness of the brand and securing coverage about Hunsk. In the coming quarter, we anticipate spending 70 hours on this strategy.

TACTICS

- Determine angle and messages for a pitch to motorcycle enthusiast publications. We believe the following story angles would resonate with the readers of these publications:

  o   "Tips for Taking a Tour on Your Hunsk." Five tips highlighting reasons that Hunsk bikes can make your road trip the best ever. (Includes list of top Hunsk accessories and recommended routes.)

  o   "Maintenance Tips from the Pros for Bikers." Position Hunsk as a subject matter expert on what bikers need most or how Hunsk owners can fix and tune up their own bikes.

  o   "Riding Free, Riding Safe: Tips to Keep You on the Road." Focus on ways that riders can maintain their freedom and stay safe.

- Develop first-draft pitch materials.
- Review materials with Hunsk executives.
- Develop second-draft pitch materials.
- Work with Hunsk vice president of marketing to secure final approvals on all materials.
- Distribute pitches and story suggestions to journalists.
- Follow up with a round of phone calls to spark journalists' interest in writing about Hunsk.
- Place a second round of phone calls.
- Recap results from discussions with journalists.

- Facilitate interviews (assuming we'll secure three to five interviews for Hunsk executives with these magazines).
- Develop recap of calls.
- Work with the journalists to ensure they have artwork to accompany the story.

STRATEGY 2: TIE HUNSK TO KEY LIFESTYLE TRENDS AND CONSUMER HABITS

The majority of Hunsk customers are college-educated, higher-income males aged thirty-five to fifty. Many of these customers are regular readers of men's lifestyle publications such as *Details*, *Esquire*, *GQ*, *Heartland USA*, *Maxim*, *Men's Journal*, *National Geographic Adventure*, *Playboy*, and *Popular Mechanics*. To secure coverage in these publications, we recommend conducting a press tour to take place in the next six weeks to educate journalists about Hunsk motorcycles and key lifestyle trends and consumer habits. We envision working approximately 140 hours to set up and conduct the tour and follow up afterward.

TACTICS

- Develop pitch materials to spark journalists' interest in sitting down with the executives of Hunsk, the maker of the finest motorcycles in the world.
- Distribute pitch to request an in-person meeting. Follow up with phone calls to set up a press tour to meet with the journalists and talk with them about Hunsk.
- Develop background materials to be shared on the press tour. Identify key trends that are driving the excitement for motorcycles.
- Facilitate the meetings with journalists and explore their interest in writing about Hunsk. Share some of our initial ideas:

  o **The Hunsk Hunks: Men of the American Roadway and Their Bikes.** Present a photo editorial of Hunsk bike owners and their machines.
  o **Live Free: Getting Away from It All.** Highlight stories about Hunsk riders, where they go, and why. (Include photo montage of various riders, places they've been, etc.)
  o **Hunsk Celebrity Bikers.** Identify a celebrity (athlete, musician, or entertainer) who is a Hunsk motorcycle aficionado for a feature story. Create an adventure campaign about the various places the person likes to ride, notable trips he's taken, etc.

- o **Biker Businessmen.** Showcase businessmen in their suits with their Hunsk bikes to resonate with potential Hunsk purchasers, and profile each of the riders, including why they're involved in motorcycling.
- o **Hunsk Style.** Focus on Hunsk bikers, and show how non-bikers can acquire the biker look.

- Provide the journalists with the names of customers for testimonials about why they love their Hunsks. Provide journalists with an opportunity to go for a ride on a Hunsk.
- Follow up with the journalists after the tour. Distribute thank-you notes and solicit feedback on the value of the meeting and their plans to write.
- Track editorial coverage and merchandise on the Hunsk Web site.

STRATEGY 3: TELL THE STORY OF HUNSK'S REINVENTION AND RETURN TO ITS ROOTS

Hunsk customers embody many of the same qualities as business leaders and entrepreneurs: they are independent, drawn to risk, and confident. Reaching out to the business media provides a twofold opportunity: to tell the story of Hunsk's reinvention and return to its roots and position of industry leader and to simultaneously connect with business leaders who are potential Hunsk riders.

We recommend reaching out to a national business publication to place a story about the company. Possible targets are *BusinessWeek, Fast Company, Fortune, Forbes, SmartMoney*, and the *Wall Street Journal*. To accomplish this strategy, we envision working 100 hours on Hunsk's behalf.

POSSIBLE STORY ANGLES

We envision developing and pitching the following stories:

- **"The Long Lonesome Highway: Hunsk Returns."** Focus on how the company has developed a core group of fans and reinvented itself by going back to its roots. Include commentary from a variety of internal and third-party sources.
- **"Celebrating a Quarter Century of Hunsk."** Present a retrospective of the company and a forward look to reinvigorate the brand. Include the perspective of the first employees, company milestones, etc.
- **"Back to School."** One way that Hunsk is making a comeback and building excitement around its brand is through a series of regional motorcycle driving schools where bike owners can pick up professional tips and tricks and let loose on the track, test-drive the latest Hunsk cycles, and convene with other Hunsk owners.

TACTICS

- Determine angle and key messages.
- Develop background pitch materials to explain key points, and include quotes from third-party influencers.
- Determine who will serve as the best executive spokesperson for this story. For instance, we believe Hunsk's CEO should serve as the executive spokesperson for the vision of the company. His history and reputation for visionary thinking gives him unique credibility and the ability to bring leadership to this issue. Hunsk's vice president of marketing can focus on the immediate operational and marketing milestones the company has recently achieved.
- Determine whether any third-party influencers are available to talk on Hunsk's behalf.
- Work with a journalist on the story.
- Consider distributing a companion press release news via Business Wire or PR Newswire the day the story breaks.
- Respond reactively to follow-up calls regarding the news.
- Facilitate interviews as necessary with tier-two publications.
- Track coverage to send to investors and employees.
- Merchandise important coverage appropriately on Hunsk's Web site regarding the transaction.

STRATEGY 4: CREATE SUPPORT FOR HUNSK ONLINE

Creating an online Hunsk community is an important element in the effort to rally a key constituency around the brand. To accomplish this, we suggest reaching out to a variety of blogs written about and by motorcycle enthusiasts. The list of appropriate blogs could include these:

- Motorcyclebloggers.com
- Motorcycle Bloggers International
- The Ride Report
- WhyBike.com

We anticipate spending 15 hours per month to create support for Hunsk online, which comes to a total of 180 hours per year.

TACTICS

- Identify top blogs, key community influencers, and online communities where motorcycle enthusiasts are gathered.
- Monitor relevant blog coverage as a means of keeping current with what's in the hearts and minds of motorcycle enthusiasts and online influencers. This will also help us understand what topics and issues are driving consumer behavior.

- Engage bloggers in a number of ways, such as commenting on what they are writing about and offering the perspective of Hunsk spokespeople when it is relevant.
- Stay top-of-mind with influential bloggers by keeping them apprised of upcoming Hunsk announcements and activities.
- Develop a point of view about what the bloggers are posting, and work with Hunsk Motorcycles to craft comments to post in response. Create the comments and send them to Hunsk's executives to post so they are engaged with the community and participate in the discussion. Monitor the blog for responses to the posts as they appear, and participate in the resulting dialogue.

STRATEGY 5: HIT THE ROAD WITH MUSEUM PARTICIPATION

To spotlight the history of the company, we would seek opportunities for vintage Hunsk models to be shown in ten exhibitions and museum displays across the United States. This type of opportunity could be leveraged to gain media coverage of the current display and history of the event. Additional opportunities for visibility would arise from taking an active role and participating in the events sponsored by the museums. The following is one such example:

"MOTOSTARS: CELEBRITIES + MOTORCYCLES"

The Motorcycle Hall of Fame Museum will spotlight more than one hundred of the world's most recognizable enthusiasts in its new exhibit, "MotoStars: Celebrities + Motorcycles." Scheduled to open in spring, the eight-thousand-square-foot exhibit will feature many priceless machines, exclusive memorabilia, and tales from celebrities' favorite two-wheeled adventures.

If Hunsk decides it would like to pursue this strategy, Communiqué PR would work to publicize the events by securing articles and calendar mentions in local and community newspapers. We envision working fifty hours to support Hunsk's PR activities at each event. This brings the total hours for this strategy to 500 hours for the year.

TACTICS

- Identify a list of ten exhibitions or museums at which to display vintage Hunsk models.
- Develop a media alert about Hunsk's participation.
- Work to gain Hunsk and the museum's approval on the alert.
- Follow up with local journalists to spark their interest in writing about the exhibition.
- Invite print and broadcast news outlets to attend the event. Encourage print media to bring a photographer.

- Develop b-roll to provide to broadcast news outlets.
- Staff the events to help ensure that journalists have a good experience as well as the opportunity to interview executives.

STRATEGY 6: PURSUE AND WIN INDUSTRY AWARDS

Awards are a superb way to reinforce positive perceptions about Hunsk. Awards provide increased visibility in the marketplace and can also position the company as a category leader. Awards can help Hunsk build credibility for its motorcycles by showing that the product is perceived as superior by independent experts. Winning awards also provides an opportunity to talk about the company and highlight the performance and the management of the company. To secure the right awards, Communiqué PR anticipates working 10 hours each month (120 hours for the year) on Hunsk's behalf and will do the following:

TACTICS FOR PURSUIT OF AWARDS

- Identify appropriate awards. We'll devote time to researching awards in the automotive, supply chain management, and retail industry sectors.
- Develop a comprehensive awards grid that will include submission deadlines.
- Complete and submit award nominations.
- Ensure that the awards won are appropriately merchandised on the Hunsk Web site and in press materials. Following is a sample list of target award opportunities we have identified for Hunsk.

SAMPLE AWARDS FOR HUNSK

Award	Description	Submission Date
MBI Award 2008 Presented by Motorcycle Bloggers International	The MBI Riders Choice awards are given for events, actions by a person or group, and new products sold for the first time during the award year. The organizers recognize the best and the worst within the motorcycling world with two awards: Star and Fallen Star. The former is for noteworthy achievement and the latter for serious lapse of judgment.	May
Supertest Awards	The Supertest competition, held at the Almeria track in Spain, is judged by fifteen journalists from publications all around the globe. The competition runs back-to-back tests for sports bikes from all the major motorcycle manufacturers.	March
Masterbike Awards	Masterbike is an independent track test for sports bikes organized by *Motociclismo*, the best-selling bike magazine in Spain, with a judging panel of sixteen international motorcycle magazines. The Masterbike test is considered one of the most important and influential magazine tests due to its impartiality and fairness.	March

BUDGET INFORMATION

Strategy	Hours	Rate	Fees
Demonstrate Hunsk's value with motorcycle enthusiasts	70	$200	$14,000
Tie Hunsk to key lifestyle trends and consumer habits	140	$200	$28,000
Tell the story of Hunsk's reinvention and return to its roots	100	$200	$20,000
Create support for Hunsk online	180	$200	$36,000
Hit the road with museum participation	500	$200	$100,000
Pursue and win industry awards	120	$200	$24,000
Total			**$222,000**

ACTIVITY TIMELINE

We envision moving forward on the strategies in the following timeframes:

Strategy	Timeline
Demonstrate Hunsk's value with motorcycle enthusiasts	Q3
Tie Hunsk to key lifestyle trends and consumer habits	Q4
Tell the Story of Hunsk's reinvention and return to its roots	Q4
Create support for Hunsk online	Ongoing
Hit the road with museum participation	Ongoing
Pursue and win industry awards	Ongoing

Once we have your feedback on this plan, we'll develop more detailed timelines that outline projected completion time for each tactic.

EXPECTED RESULTS—MEASUREMENT OF SUCCESS

Following are our expected results for the six strategies outlined above.

Strategy 1: Demonstrate Hunsk's value with motorcycle enthusiasts.

- Build relationships with ten journalists with magazines written for motorcycle enthusiasts.
- Secure three positive articles about Hunsk and its bikes.

Strategy 2: Tie Hunsk to key lifestyle trends and consumer habits.

- Secure meetings with a minimum of fifteen journalists with consumer lifestyle publications.
- Spark the interest of five journalists in writing about Hunsk. (Because many of the consumer lifestyle publications are long-lead, we wouldn't anticipate articles to appear for at least six months.)

Strategy 3: Tell the story of Hunsk's reinvention and return to its roots.

- Place a significant feature story on Hunsk in a national news publication.

Strategy 4: Create support for Hunsk online.

- Engage at least five bloggers a month and motivate them to write in a meaningful way about Hunsk.
- Establish relationships with a total of thirty-five to forty-five bloggers for the year.

Strategy 5: Hit the road with museum participation.
- Secure a minimum of ten articles about Hunsk events around the country.
- Ensure that for each event at least one local print or broadcast story about Hunsk will appear.

Strategy 6: Pursue and win industry awards.
- Complete one or two award nominations a month.
- Win at least five awards for the company and its motorcycles in 2008.

CONCLUSION

We are eager to receive your feedback on this plan and hope it provides a detailed road map of our proposed activity. Please feel free to contact me with any questions. I may be reached at name@communiquepr.com or at (555) 555-5555, ext. 123.

NOTES

INTRODUCTION

1. Strategic Public Relations Center, Annenberg School of Communication, University of Southern California. "Public Relations Generally Accepted Practices (G.A.P.) Study II (2003 Data): Section 2: Executive Summary."
2. Pingdom, "How we got from 1 to 162 million websites on the internet" (April 4, 2008).
3. "News Audiences Increasingly Politicized," The Pew Research Center for the People & the Press (June 8, 2004).
4. Todd Shields, "Sirius-XM Merger Approval May Hinge Upon FCC's Tate (Update 2)," Bloomberg.com News.
5. HD Radio press release, "Best Buy Expands HD Digital Radio Line-Up at All Stores Nationwide," (April 23, 2007).
6. National Consumers League, "American Consumers' Definition of the Socially Responsible Company Runs Counter to Established Beliefs," *NCL News* (May 31, 2006).
7. Council of Public Relations Firms. "Resources: Industry Facts."
8. U.S Department of Labor, Bureau of Labor Statistics. *Occupational Outlook Handbook, 2004-05 Edition.*
9. Michael Dell, commencement address, University of Texas at Austin, June 2003.

THE CASE FOR A STRATEGIC APPROACH TO PR

1. Council of Public Relations Firms. "Resources: Industry Facts."
2. Michael Levine, *Guerrilla P.R.* (New York, HarperCollins, 1993).
3. Sunzi Sun Tzu, *The Art of War.* (New York, Courier Dover Publications 2002).
4. Jack Myers, *Jack Myers Media Business Report,* "Advertising and Marketing Communications Forecast, 2006-2009," JackMyers.com, September 15, 2007.
5. Al Ries and Laura Ries, *The Fall of Advertising and the Rise of PR,* (New York, HarperCollins, 2002).
6. John Wolfe, "PR Steals the Spotlight," *The Advertiser* (December 2006).
7. Robin D. Rusch, "Is Advertising Effective in Brand Building?" brandchannel.com (January 2003).
8. "Turbo Tax Rap Contest Draws Hundreds of Videos," *PROMO Magazine* (April 16, 2007).
9. "Women Harley Riders," *Road & Travel Magazine,* 2005.
10. Steve Kayser, "PR vs. Advertising: 3 Facts of Life," Tech Image PR Intelligence Report (September 7, 2005).
11. "The Engine that Fueled Vespa's Turnaround," *The Advertiser* (December 2006).
12. Eleanor Trickett, "Great Moments in Consumer PR," *PRWeek* (August 14, 2006).
13. Patagonia, Inc. "Corporate Social Responsibility," *The Footprint Chronicles* (November 2007).
14. Joe Truini, "Tending the Great Outdoors: Retailer practices, preaches environmental sustainability," *Waste News* (October 29, 2007).
15. Tricia Duryee, "Seattle's Tegic Sold in $265M Cash Deal," *The Seattle Times* (June 22, 2007).
16. "CEOs Rely Most on Public Relations Professionals for Reputation Management; CEO Survey Reveals Public Relations' Growing Corporate Role," *Business Wire* (November 12, 2004).

PRINCIPLE 1: SELL PR TO KEY STAKEHOLDERS WITHIN YOUR COMPANY

1. Doris Kearns Goodwin, *Team of Rivals* (New York, Simon and Schuster, 2006).
2. Roger Fisher, William Ury, and Bruce Patton, *Getting to Yes* (New York, Penguin Books, 1991).
3. Ibid.

PRINCIPLE 2: SELECT YOUR PR TEAM WISELY

1. Council of Public Relations Firms, *Hiring a Public Relations Firm: A Guide for Clients* (New York, Council of Public Relations Firms, 2000).

PRINCIPLE 3: KNOW YOUR TARGET AUDIENCES AND HOW TO REACH THEM

1. Chris Anderson, "Sorry PR People, You're Blocked," *The Long Tail*, October 29, 2007.
2. "Number of U.S. Daily Newspapers," *Facts About Newspapers: A statistical summary of the newspaper industry, 2004*, Newspaper Association of America (2004).
3. "U.S. Daily Newspaper Circulation," *Facts About Newspapers: A statistical summary of the newspaper industry, 2004*, Newspaper Association of America (2004).
4. "Striking the Right Print/Online Balance," *CONTENTBLOGGER*, Shore Communications, November 15, 2004.
5. Susan Harrow, "5 Tips to Getting Booked on *Oprah*," *Sixty Second Secrets*, Issue No. 22.
6. Erica Iacono, "TV Newsmagazine Genre Faces Challenges," *PRWeek*, November 15, 2006.
7. "Deloitte's State of the Media Democracy Survey—Rethink What You Know," January 18, 2008, www.deloitte.com.

PRINCIPLE 4: LEVERAGE EMERGING TRENDS AND TECHNOLOGIES

1. "Internet Usage Statistics," *Internet World Stats: Usage and Population Statistics*, March 2008.
2. Paul M. Rand and Giovanni Rodriguez, "Relating to the Public: The Evolving Role of Public Relations in the Age of Social Media," Council of Public Relations Firms white paper, 2007.
3. Nielsen *BuzzMetrics*, "CGM Overview," 2008, www.nielsenbuzzmetrics.com.
4. Dan Frost, "Using the Web to Draw in Crowds," *The New York Times*, May 21, 2008.
5. Tom Zeller, Jr. "Gaming the Search Engine, in a Political Season," *The New York Times*, November 6, 2006.
6. Ibid.

7.   Ibid.
8.   Dave Sifry, "State of the Blogosphere, April 2006 Part 2: On Language and Tagging (May 1, 2006) http://technorati.com.
9.   Amanda Lenhart, Deborah Fellows and John Horrigan. "Content Creation Online," *Reports: Online Activities & Pursuits*, Pew Internet & American Life Project (July 7, 2008),
10. Larry Weber, "Social Media Returns PR to Its Roots," *PRWeek* (August 19, 2007).
11. Rick Miller, "It's Time to Get Social-Media Savvy," *PRWeek* (April 2, 2007).
12. Frank Washkuch, "State of Transition," *PRWeek* (March 30, 2008).
13. Frank Ahrens, "Gannett to Change Its Papers' Approach, *The Washington Post* (November 7, 2006).
14. Andrew Gordon, "Google Carves New Path by Blogging to Confront Issues," *PRWeek*, October 10, 2005.
15. Andrew Gordon, "Sun Embraces Blogging, Bounces Back," *PRWeek*, January 30, 2006.
16. The Blog Council, "Corporate Bloggers Launch the 'Blog Council' Organization," December 6, 2007.
17. Mary Madden, "Online Video," *Reports: Technology & Media*, Pew Internet & American Life Project, July 25, 2007,
18. Mary Madden, "Podcast Downloading," *Reports: Online Activities & Pursuits*, Pew Internet & American Life Project, November 22, 2006,
19. Michael Bush, "Home Depot Launches Social-Media Initiative," *PRWeek* (December 6, 2007).
20. "Social Networking Sites Grow 47 Percent, Year Over Year, Reaching 45 Percent of Web Users," Nielsen/NetRatings, May 11, 2006.
21. Jeremiah Owyang, "Social Network Stats: Facebook, MySpace, Reunion," *Web Strategy by Jeremiah*, January 9, 2008.
22. Michael Arrington, "iLike: By Far the Most Popular Facebook Application," *TechCrunch* (May 25, 2007).
23. Clement James, "Sun Sets Up Shop in Second Life Virtual World," *iTnews*, October 12, 2006.
24. Celeste Altus, "Brave New World," *PRWeek* (October 30, 2006).
25. Ibid.
26. "More Than Half of MySpace Visitors Are Now Age 35 or Older, as the Site's Demographic Composition Continues to Shift," comScore press release, October 5, 2006.
27. Louise Story, "Outcome of an Ad Contest Starts an Uproar on YouTube," *The New York Times* (June 27, 2007).

28. Julie Bosman, "Chevy Tries a Write-Your-Own-Ad Approach, and the Potshots Fly," *The New York Times* (April 4, 2006).
29. Victoria Grantham, "Disclosure Critical in Blogosphere," *PRWeek* (July 23, 2007).
30. Hamilton Nolan, "Edelman Apologizes for Wal-Mart Blog Disclosure Omission," *PRWeek* (October 18, 2006).
31. "White Paper: Tips for Effective Word of Mouth Marketing," gL Market Research, November 2007.
32. Keith O'Brien, "Web 2.0 Environment Must Let Companies Have a Voice, Too," *PRWeek* (February 1, 2007).

PRINCIPLE 5: DEVELOP A STRATEGIC PR PLAN

1. Simona Covel, "Paying for PR—but Only When It Works," *The Wall Street Journal* (2008).
2. Christian Caple, "WSU Tops UW in Apple Cup Thriller," *The Daily*, University of Washington (November 26, 2007).
3. Al Reis and Jack Trout, *Marketing Warfare* (New York: McGraw-Hill, 1986).
4. Erica Iacono, "Contest Keeps Ball Park Top of Mind During BBQ Season," *PRWeek* (September 6, 2006).
5. David Weinberger, "Authenticity: Is It Real or Is It Marketing?" *Harvard Business Review*, HBR Interactive Study, 2008.

PRINCIPLE 6: CRAFT A COMPELLING STORY

1. Peter Guber, "The Four Truths of the Storyteller," *Harvard Business Review*, December 2007.
2. Mark Turner, *Literary Mind: The Origins of Thought and Language* (New York: Oxford University Press, 1996).
3. Stephen Denning, *The Springboard: How Storytelling Ignites Action in Knowledge-Era Organizations* (Boston: Butterworth-Heinemann, 2000).
4. Peter Guber, "The Four Truths."
5. "Sweat365 Unveils a New Online Social Network Targeted Toward Everyday Athletes," Reuters, January 4, 2008.
6. Peter Guber, "The Four Truths."
7. Melvin Mencher, *News Reporting and Writing* (New York: McGraw-Hill, 1999).
8. David B. Yoffie and Mary Kwak, *Judo Strategy: Turning Your Competitors' Strength to Your Advantage* (Boston: Harvard Business School Publishing Corporation, 2001).

9. Peter Guber, "The Four Truths."
10. Gerry Spence, *Win Your Case: How to Present, Persuade, and Prevail—Every Place, Every Time* (New York: St. Martin's Press, 2005).
11. Anne Lamott, *Bird by Bird: Some Instructions on Writing and Life* (New York: Pantheon Books, 1994).

PRINCIPLE 7: BUILD MEDIA RELATIONSHIPS FOR STRATEGIC ADVANTAGE

1. Robert Ailes, *You Are the Message: Getting What You Want by Being Who You Are* (New York: Doubleday, 1988).
2. Ibid.

PRINCIPLE 8: MAINTAIN AN OPEN INFORMATION FLOW

1. Starbucks 2007 10-K.
2. Sarah D. Scalet, "The Five Most Shocking Things About the ChoicePoint Data Security Breach," *CSO Magazine* (May 1, 2005).
3. Erica Iacono, "LexisNexis Quick to Respond to Seisint Security Breach," *PRWeek* (March 15, 2005).
4. Allen H. Center and Patrick Jackson, *Public Relations Practices: Managerial Case Studies and Problems*, Sixth Edition (Upper Saddle River, New Jersey: Prentice Hall, 2003).

PRINCIPLE 9: MEASURE AND MERCHANDIZE YOUR RESULTS

1. Keith O'Brien, "On the Right Track," *PRWeek*, October 9, 2006.
2. Council of Public Relations Firms, *PR Measurement Report*, sponsored by the Seventh Annual Strategic Public Relations Conference (Chicago: Lawrence Ragan Communications, 2002).
3. Ibid.
4. Michael F. Roizen and Mehmet C. Oz, *You: Staying Young: The Owner's Manual for Extending Your Warranty* (New York: Free Press, 2007).
5. Mark Weiner, *Unleashing the Power of PR: A Contrarian's Guide to Marketing and Communication* (San Francisco: Jossey-Bass, 2006).
6. Tim Armstrong, "The Flip Side of Fear: Marketing to the Empowered Consumer," *ASIS&T Bulletin* (December 2005/January 2006).
7. Analysis of Ford Motor and Bridgestone stock value and market capitalization from Aug. 2000 through Oct. 2002.

PRINCIPLE 10: KEEP YOUR PR PROGRAM
RELEVANT OVER TIME

1. Malcolm Gladwell, *The Tipping Point: How Little Things Can Make a Big Difference* (Boston: Little, Brown, 2000).
2. Sun Tzu. *The Art of War.*

APPENDIX

1. David Weinberger, "Authenticity."

INDEX

C

D

E

F

G